Genetic Engineering

Other Books of Related Interest:

Opposing Viewpoints Series

Adoption

America in the Twenty-First Century

Biomedical Ethics

The Environment

Food

Genetic Engineering

Health

Humanity's Future

Technology and Society

Current Controversies Series

Biodiversity

Conserving the Environment

Ethics

Genetic Engineering

Medical Ethics

At Issue Series

Cloning

The Ethics of Genetic Engineering

The Ethics of Human Cloning

Food Safety

Gene Therapy

Genetically Engineered Foods

Human Embryo Experimentation

Reproductive Technology

Genetic Engineering

Sylvia Engdahl, Book Editor

GREENHAVEN PRESS
An imprint of Thomson Gale, a part of The Thomson Corporation

Detroit • New York • San Francisco • San Diego • New Haven, Conn.
Waterville, Maine • London • Munich

Bonnie Szumski, *Publisher*
Helen Cothran, *Managing Editor*
David M. Haugen, *Series Editor*

© 2006 Thomson Gale, a part of The Thomson Corporation.

Thomson and Star Logo are trademarks and Gale and Greenhaven Press are registered trademarks used herein under license.

For more information, contact:
Greenhaven Press
27500 Drake Rd.
Farmington Hills, MI 48331-3535
Or you can visit our Internet site at http://www.gale.com

LIBRARY OF CONGRESS CATALOGING-IN-PUBLICATION DATA

Genetic engineering / Sylvia Engdahl, book editor
    p. cm. -- (Contemporary issues companion)
    Includes bibliographical references and index.
    0-7377-3255-5 (lib. : alk. paper) 0-7377-3256-3 (pbk. : alk. paper)
    1. Genetic engineering. I. Engdahl, Sylvia Louise. II. Series.
    QH442.G4414 2006
    306.4'6--dc22

                                                        2005055051

Printed in the United States of America
10 9 8 7 6 5 4 3 2 1

Contents

Chapter 3: Genetic Enhancement of Human Abilities

Foreword

In the news, on the streets, and in neighborhoods, individuals are confronted with a variety of social problems. Such problems may affect people directly: A young woman may struggle with depression, suspect a friend of having bulimia, or watch a loved one battle cancer. And even the issues that do not directly affect her private life—such as religious cults, domestic violence, or legalized gambling—still impact the larger society in which she lives. Discovering and analyzing the complexities of issues that encompass communal and societal realms as well as the world of personal experience is a valuable educational goal in the modern world.

Effectively addressing social problems requires familiarity with a constantly changing stream of data. Becoming well informed about today's controversies is an intricate process that often involves reading myriad primary and secondary sources, analyzing political debates, weighing various experts' opinions—even listening to firsthand accounts of those directly affected by the issue. For students and general observers, this can be a daunting task because of the sheer volume of information available in books, periodicals, on the evening news, and on the Internet. Researching the consequences of legalized gambling, for example, might entail sifting through congressional testimony on gambling's societal effects, examining private studies on Indian gaming, perusing numerous Web sites devoted to Internet betting, and reading essays written by lottery winners as well as interviews with recovering compulsive gamblers. Obtaining valuable information can be time-consuming—since it often requires researchers to pore over numerous documents and commentaries before discovering a source relevant to their particular investigation.

Greenhaven's Contemporary Issues Companion series seeks to assist this process of research by providing readers with useful and pertinent information about today's complex issues. Each volume in this anthology series focuses on a topic of current interest, presenting informative and thought-provoking selections written from a wide variety of viewpoints. The readings selected by the editors include such diverse sources as personal accounts and case studies, pertinent factual and statistical articles, and relevant commentaries and overviews. This diversity of sources and views, found in every Contemporary Issues Companion, offers readers a broad perspective in one convenient volume.

In addition, each title in the Contemporary Issues Companion series is designed especially for young adults. The selections included in every volume are chosen for their accessibility and are expertly edited in consideration of both the reading and comprehension levels of the audience. The structure of the anthologies also enhances accessibility. An introductory essay places each issue in context and provides helpful facts such as historical background or current statistics and legislation that pertain to the topic. The chapters that follow organize the material and focus on specific aspects of the book's topic. Every essay is introduced by a brief summary of its main points and biographical information about the author. These summaries aid in comprehension and can also serve to direct readers to material of immediate interest and need. Finally, a comprehensive index allows readers to efficiently scan and locate content.

The Contemporary Issues Companion series is an ideal launching point for research on a particular topic. Each anthology in the series is composed of readings taken from an extensive gamut of resources, including periodicals, newspapers, books, government documents, the publications of private and public organizations, and Internet Web sites. In these volumes, readers will find factual support suitable for use in reports, debates, speeches, and research papers. The anthologies also facilitate further research, featuring a book and periodical bibliography and a list of organizations to contact for additional information.

A perfect resource for both students and the general reader, Greenhaven's Contemporary Issues Companion series is sure to be a valued source of current, readable information on social problems that interest young adults. It is the editors' hope that readers will find the Contemporary Issues Companion series useful as a starting point to formulate their own opinions about and answers to the complex issues of the present day.

Introduction

Many people think of genes as separate units that independently control inheritance of specific characteristics. That was the view proposed by Gregor Mendel in the nineteenth century and accepted as true by other scientists at the beginning of the twentieth century—genes were "units of inheritance" on which Mendel's laws of heredity depended. It was a revolutionary view because science had previously assumed that inheritance involved some sort of blending of parents' characteristics rather than the transmission of discrete entities and that inheritance of characteristics acquired during a parent's lifetime was possible. The Mendelian concept of genes led to great advances in understanding how inherited traits are passed from one generation to the next.

It soon became apparent, however, that genetic inheritance is more complicated. Early in the twentieth century, scientists demonstrated that some genes are linked to other genes and that some genes modify the action of others. Gradually, more was learned about the mechanisms of genetics, and in 1953 James Watson and Francis Crick discovered the molecular structure of DNA (deoxyribonucleic acid), the chemical of which genes are composed. This made it possible to physically identify individual genes. As molecular genetics progressed, more and more emphasis was placed on the function of genes; scientists viewed them not as mere units of inheritance but as "blueprints" for the production of the proteins that control the biological functioning of living organisms on an ongoing basis. Biologists recognized that genes are responsible not only for passing on traits, but for controlling an organism's body throughout its lifetime.

The entire assembly of genes possessed by an organism—its genome—is present in every cell of its body except the germ cells (egg or sperm cells). Because cells have different functions and the conditions under which they function change over time, most genes in any given cell at a given time are not expressed—that is, they are "turned off." In the 1970s geneticists learned that some genes are regulators of other genes; their function is not to produce proteins but to turn other genes off and on. Scientists also learned that humans and chimpanzees are at least 98.5 percent genetically identical. Something other than the simple presence or absence of specific genes must therefore account for the obvious difference between humans and chimps, and geneticists believe that regulator genes have a great deal to do with that difference. The process, however, has yet to be fully explained, as science still has much to learn about gene expression.

Many geneticists theorize that the pattern of gene interaction, not merely the collection of individual genes, determines an organism's characteristics. This view was strengthened by the completion of the Human Genome Project in 2003, which revealed that the human genome consists of only about thirty thousand genes instead of the more than one hundred thousand that had been expected. Nevertheless, the general public still thinks in terms of separate genes as the carriers of individual traits, as do many scientists who are not specialists in molecular genetics. Nearly fifty years ago the eminent evolutionary biologist Ernst Mayr criticized this view, calling it "beanbag genetics" because it suggested that genetic change is like adding or subtracting individual beans to or from a bag. Although beanbag genetics as an overall concept no longer has defenders among those knowledgeable about recent developments in genomics (the study of the role played by genes, and the proteins they produce, in the body's biochemical processes), the fact that individual genes can be added to a genome through recombinant DNA technology gives superficial support to the idea that they are independent. With that technology, on which genetic engineering is based, bacteria and plants—and in some cases animals—can now be given genes that provide potential benefits. Because a very few human diseases are indeed caused by the presence or absence of single genes, doctors hope that in the future these diseases can be cured by gene therapy. However, as a general rule, making genetic changes to animals would not be that simple.

Most genetically based illnesses—and certainly most if not all other biological characteristics—are dependent on more than one gene, and some genes affect more than one characteristic. As psychologist Steven Pinker explains in his 2002 book *The Blank Slate*, "In a complex organism, one gene may turn on a second one, which speeds up the activity of a third one (but only if a fourth one is active), which then turns off the original gene (but only if a fifth one is inactive), and so on." Furthermore, not only their interactions but environmental factors have a role in determining whether specific genes are expressed. Therefore, geneticists caution against speaking of "a gene for" any particular trait, desirable or undesirable, as both proponents and opponents of genetic engineering tend to do. Some scientists believe that in the foreseeable future, the interactions between genes and the processes by which they are turned on and off will be thoroughly enough understood to make extensive genetic engineering of higher organisms possible. Others believe that the complexity of the patterns involved is so great that no such prediction can be made.

Most of the controversy surrounding genetic engineering ignores this issue, focusing instead on whether particular advances in genetic engineering would be a good thing or a bad thing if accomplished. It is often assumed that their accomplishment, if not banned, is a foregone conclusion. But it may be that neither the hopes of proponents nor the fears of opponents will be realized in the twenty-first century, if ever. No one yet knows. What *is* known is that the more science learns about genomics, the more complicated the expression of genes proves to be.

The extent to which human characteristics are determined by genes has long been a hotly debated issue. For some time it has been generally agreed that both genes ("nature") and environment ("nurture") play important roles. Now the science of genomics is shedding new light on the way in which the two are related. "The discovery of how genes actually influence human behavior, and how human behavior influences genes, is about to recast the debate entirely. No longer is it nature versus nurture but nature via nurture," says science writer Matt Ridley in his 2003 book *Nature Via Nurture*. "The more we lift the lid on the genome, the more vulnerable to [an organism's] experience genes appear to be." He states, "By far the most important discovery of recent years in brain science is that genes are at the mercy of actions as well as vice versa. The . . . genes that run learning and memory are not just the cause of behavior; they are also the consequence. . . . [They] are designed to be switched on and off by events."

In terms of human genetic modification, both advocates and critics assume that simply inserting genes for desired traits into unborn babies would control what characteristics the children would develop. As genomics has shown, though, there is much more involved than that; "designing" future humans would require inserted genes to be expressed and to interact properly with the entire genome. Thus, if an organism's response to experience influences the expression of its genes, then genetic engineering of any but the most primitive life forms will determine less about their development than is usually imagined. Understanding this will likely influence the shape of the debate concerning the future prospects and applications of genetic engineering for years to come.

CHAPTER 1

Genetic Engineering in Agriculture and Industry

The Benefits of Genetically Modified Food Outweigh the Risks

Radley Balko

Radley Balko is a freelance writer and editor who lives in Arlington, Virginia. He is a policy analyst for the Cato Institute, a libertarian public policy research foundation. In the following selection, he argues that genetically modified food is needed to feed the world's population, and that rejecting it on the basis of potential harm is being overcautious. He explains that critics of genetically modified food often invoke the "precautionary principle," a rule commonly advocated by environmentalists, which maintains that until it is certain what effects a technological development will have, it should be avoided. In Balko's opinion, to apply that rule to genetic modification of food would cause known harm by allowing the people of impoverished nations to starve unnecessarily.

According to recent reports, the world may soon be out of bananas. Because of the starchy fruit's unique method of reproduction, it seems, banana plantations in Africa, Asia and Central America are uniquely susceptible to fungi, viruses and pests. Unless scientists can find a way to genetically enhance the banana's ability to ward off parasites, we could be banana-less in ten years.

Several agroscience companies believe they can genetically engineer such an invincible banana by copying parts of the genetic codes of other fruits and instilling them into the banana. The problem? Increasing opposition from environmental activists and some governments to genetic meddling with nature.

The banana crisis provides a nice jumping off point for a discussion on the general costs and benefits of genetically modified organisms. What potential harm could be done by the "new banana?" How likely are these harms? And, considering that the banana is a dietary staple for entire populations of people in some parts of Africa and the Caribbean, what are the costs of not assembling a new, improved superbanana?

Genetically Modified Food Is Now Common

By most estimates, up to 70% of the processed foods at your local grocery store contain at least one ingredient that's been genetically altered. That is, certain genetic attributes not native to the food have been "cut" from the DNA of other organisms and "pasted" into, for example, your strawberries. Such modifications are usually done to enhance the things we like about certain foods—their nutritional content, for example, or how long they can stay fresh without spoiling, or their brilliant color. Modification can also enable crops to emit their own insecticides to ward off pests, or to cause plants to yield more grain per plant on less land, or with less water, or in less fertile soil.

But the practice of genetically modifying our foodstuffs isn't without its critics. And these critics also raise some important questions. How safe are foods that have been modified? Have the health effects of these modifications been tested? What are the risks involved? What are the benefits?

Modern agroscience has produced some astonishing innovations in the last several years. We now have grains and cereals that can tolerate early frosts, acidic soil, and drought. A 1999 study published in the journal *Nature Biotechnology* found that 96.2 percent of genetically modified (GM) plants could survive freezing experiments, versus just 9.5 percent of unaltered plants. When subjected to drought conditions three-fourths of the GM plants survived, compared with just two percent of the traditional plants.

We now have strawberries, bananas, raspberries and melons that can stay ripe on the shelves for days longer than their natural forbearers. We can even grow plants that have been bioengineered to absorb toxic metals from the soil, enabling land tainted by mercury or lead, for example, to be usable again for agriculture.

Variations on maize and corn are under development right now that would make each plant yield kernels more substantive and suited for livestock, meaning cows and pigs and chickens would require less feed, meaning we'd need less land to produce more meat.

Scientists are also looking at ways of applying the leavening characteristics of wheat bread to other grains, such as rice or maize.

There's even research underway to grow foods for human consumption that are engineered to deliver vaccines and medication, enabling them to both nourish and medically treat the poorest areas of the world.

What Are the Risks?

Critics of bioengineered agriculture, however, point out that such breakthroughs don't come without costs. They argue that tampering with the genetic makeup of plants can have unforeseen consequences, such as the offspring of "super weeds" resistant to herbicides. They say it's possible that plants emitting their own toxins could cause natural pests to mutate into bigger, stronger, more resistant bugs.

Critics also say that not enough tests have been done on the health effects such foods can have on humans, particularly over the long term. They worry about hidden allergens. If an apple, for example, is embedded with part of the genetic code of a peanut, might those with severe peanut allergies be adversely affected by eating that apple? And should that apple be labeled to warn them of the possibility?

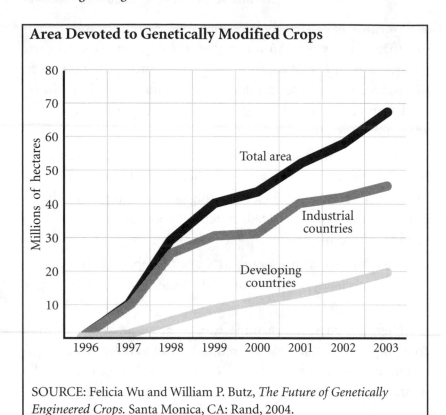

Area Devoted to Genetically Modified Crops

SOURCE: Felicia Wu and William P. Butz, *The Future of Genetically Engineered Crops.* Santa Monica, CA: Rand, 2004.

A final concern involves "genetic pollution" or cross-contamination. GM foods opponents worry that pollen from genetically modified fields will eventually find its way to organic crops, and even to wild plants, potentially creating untested and unpredictable strains of plant life.

Because of these concerns, critics of genetically modified foods—which include Greenpeace, the Green Party, the World Wildlife Fund, and the European Union, among others—argue that public policy ought to follow the "precautionary principle," an edict long used by environmental advocates that states, simply, "better safe than sorry."

With respect to bioengineered agriculture, the precautionary principle says, "we aren't yet sure what kinds of effects these foods could have on humans, on similar plants, or on the environment. Until we're sure, they should be avoided."

At the very least, they say, genetically altered foods should be labeled, so that those who wish to avoid the unnecessary risks associated with them can. The European Union requires such labeling, and [in 2002] the state of Oregon . . . voted down a ballot initiative calling for similar measures.

Critics note the once widespread use of DDT, a pest killer that proved so effective at fighting malaria and typhus, it was put into use as a general insecticide. By the 1950s, they point out, DDT was found even in human breast milk. DDT was also blamed for the thinning eggshells of dozens of bird species, including the bald eagle. It was banned from public use in 1972.

Critics cite DDT as an example of how failure to embrace the precautionary principle—how forging ahead with new innovations without first weighing their potential harms—can lead to catastrophic and unforeseen consequences.

The Risks of Not Embracing GM Technology

Proponents of GM foods counter that we can never be 100% sure of a new innovation's safety. And if we applied this most extreme interpretation of the precautionary principle to every scientific breakthrough before it was implemented, we'd never move forward as a society. Pointing out that nearly all innovation carries some risk, Steve Milloy, editor of the website Junk Science, said of a GM foods critic, "if [he] had been around in prehistoric times, he would have discouraged the use of fire."

GM foods proponents point out that a panoply of respected health and environmental organizations have already signed off on the technology's safety, including the U.S. Department of Agriculture, the Food and Drug Administration, the Environmental Protection Agency, the American Medical Association, the National Academy of Sciences and the World

Health Organization. What's more, the very fact that 70% of the processed foods Americans eat are bioengineered—and that there's yet to be a major public health incident traceable to genetic modification—is testimony to their safety.

Proponents of GM foods also apply a modified version of the precautionary principle to GM foods as they relate to the current world population dynamics. It works like this: Because of the rapidly escalating populations in poor countries with little farmland, because there are more mouths to feed and precious little land to do it, and because we'd like to preserve what few untouched lands that are left (the rain forests, for example), we can't afford to not look for new ways to grow more food on less land. We need to embrace new technologies immediately, or face calamitous repercussions.

Inaction Can Be Riskier than Action

In other words, inaction often carries more risk of harm than action. Not moving ahead with technological innovations has costs. "Better safe than sorry" is still good advice. But in this case, "safe" means exploring new ways to feed more people on less land. "Sorry" means standing idly by while people go hungry, even when potential remedies are within reach.

A good example of how aversion to new technology can cause suffering occurred in Zambia. That African nation has been battling a drought for years now. Without outside help, almost 3 million Zambians face starvation. But—in following the lead of Europe—the Zambian government recently turned down 18,000 tons of emergency grain from the U.S., for the sole reason that the food had been altered genetically. Some reports even suggest that European Union officials "leaned on" the Zambian government to turn down the aid, and let its people starve. . . .

U.S. agriculture has made tremendous strides over the last century, thanks in large part to the very types of technologies proponents of the precautionary principle have long opposed.

In 1942, U.S. farms produced 56 million tons of corn on 77 million hectares of land. In 2000, they produced 252 million tons on just 29 million hectares. That's nearly a five-fold increase in just 60 years.

Feeding 7 Billion People

By the end of the new century, the earth's population of 7 billion is expected to swell to 12 billion. The International Food Policy Research Institute estimates that as much as 90% of future agricultural production will need to come from land already being used for farming.

In other words, we need to figure out ways to get more food from the same plots of land. If we don't, the growing population will need to be fed from land that's currently covered in forests, meaning less habitat for wildlife, and less biodiversity.

In his book [*The Precautionary Principle*, economist Indur M.] Goklany estimates that if global agricultural productivity were able to increase between just 1 and 1.5 percent each year, we'd actually need 98 million fewer acres of croplands over the next century to feed a bigger and wealthier population.

Emerging GM technology, proponents argue, can easily push productivity up that 1 to 1.5 percent, if not significantly higher. And many farmers can accomplish higher rates of productivity without the use of insecticides and herbicides that many of these same environmentalists oppose.

Failing to Feed People

Most GM proponents predict that if we don't figure out new ways to get more food from less land, the most likely victims won't be the activists in wealthy countries who are most opposed to GM foods development, but rather the poor and impoverished people of the third world, those most likely to feel the first effects of a world population too large to sustain itself.

In his book *Bountiful Harvest*, Dr. Thomas R. DeGregori quotes the African scientist Florence Wambugu, director of an organization attempting to bring biotechnology to Africa. Wambugu says that opposition to GM foods is a "northern luxury," reserved for those who already have plenty to eat. "The biggest risk in Africa is doing nothing," she says, "I appreciate ethical concerns, but anything that doesn't help feed our children is unethical."

Back to Bananas

The question, then, is this: Is the banana worth saving, even if we need to tamper with its genetics to do so? (Many of the world's poor depend upon the banana as a part of their diets.) Perhaps there are risks to such an endeavor, though none have yet been conclusively identified. But there's a risk to not meddling with the banana, too. That risk—which most scientists agree is almost certain to happen—is a world without bananas. And a world without bananas is a world without banana bread, banana pudding, and banana splits. More importantly, it means millions of people who live in communities that depend on bananas for trade and sustenance will soon find themselves without a dietary and financial staple. It means more poverty and, probably, more famine.

That's what's important to remember when we're debating about the future of genetically modified foods and agroscience technology: For all the yet-to-be-proven costs and unidentified harms that could potentially result from genetic modification, there also exist a number of certain, identifiable, and easily-proven harms that come from not embracing new technology, too.

Genetically Modified Crops Are Harmful

Jeffrey M. Smith

*In the following selection Jeffrey M. Smith contends that geneti-
cally modified (GM) crops pose a number of dangers to people
who eat them and to those who live near fields where they are
grown. Smith claims that animals fed GM foods in experiments
suffered countless ailments, including liver problems and sterility.
According to Smith, many scientists are worried that the genes
inserted into GM crops may enter gut bacteria, where they could
switch on dormant viruses or generate mutations. What is more,
he argues, evidence from the Philippines indicates that people
living next to GM cornfields experience skin, intestinal, and respiratory problems while the corn is pollinating. While GM foods
obviously pose a grave danger to human health, no federal agency
in the United States is monitoring the safety of these products,
Smith maintains. Jeffrey M. Smith is author of* Seeds of Decep-
tion: Exposing Industry and Government Lies About the Safety
of the Genetically Engineered Foods You're Eating.*

In a study in the early 1990's, rats were fed genetically modified (GM) tomatoes. Well actually, the rats refused to eat
them. They were force-fed. Several of the rats developed stom-
ach lesions and seven out of forty died within two weeks. Scientists at the FDA [Food and Drug Administration] who re-
viewed the study agreed that it did not provide a
demonstration of reasonable certainty of no harm. In fact,
agency scientists warned that GM foods in general might create unpredicted allergies, toxins, antibiotic-resistant diseases,
and nutritional problems. Internal FDA memos made public
from a lawsuit reveal that the scientists urged their superiors

Jeffrey M. Smith, "Genetically Engineered Foods May Pose National Health Risk,"
www.seedsofdeception.com. Reproduced by permission.

to require long-term safety testing to catch these hard-to-detect side effects. But FDA political appointees, including a former attorney for [chemical giant] Monsanto in charge of policy, ignored the scientists' warnings. The FDA does not require safety studies. Instead, if the makers of the GM foods claim that they are safe, the agency has no further questions. The GM tomato was approved in 1994.

Unpredictable Consequences

According to a July 27 [2004] report from the US National Academy of Sciences (NAS), the current system of blanket approval of GM foods by the FDA might not detect unintended changes in the composition of the food. The process of gene insertion, according to the NAS, could damage the host's DNA with unpredicted consequences. The Indian Council of Medical Research (ICMR), which released its findings a few days earlier, identified a long list of potentially dangerous side effects from GM foods that are not being evaluated. The ICMR called for a complete overhaul of existing regulations.

The safety studies conducted by the biotech industry are often dismissed by critics as superficial and designed to avoid finding problems. Tragically, scientists who voice their criticism, and those who have discovered incriminating evidence, have been threatened, stripped of responsibilities, denied funding or tenure, or fired. For example, a UK [United Kingdom] government-funded study demonstrated that rats fed a GM potato developed potentially pre-cancerous cell growth, damaged immune systems, partial atrophy of the liver, and inhibited development of their brains, livers and testicles. When the lead scientist went public with his concerns, he was promptly fired from his job after 35 years and silenced with threats of a lawsuit.

GM Soy Is Not Safe

Americans eat genetically modified foods every day. Although the GM tomato has been taken off the market, millions of acres of soy, corn, canola, and cotton have had foreign genes inserted into their DNA. The new genes allow the crops to survive applications of herbicide, create their own pesticide, or both. While there are only a handful of published animal safety studies, mounting evidence, which needs to be followed up, suggests that these foods are not safe.

Rats fed GM corn had problems with blood cell formation. Those fed GM soy had problems with liver cell formation, and the livers of rats fed GM canola were heavier. Pigs fed GM corn on several Midwest farms developed false pregnancies or sterility. Cows fed GM corn in Germany died mysteriously. And twice the number of chickens died when fed GM corn compared to those fed natural corn.

Soon after GM soy was introduced to the UK, soy allergies skyrocketed by 50 percent. Without follow-up tests, we can't be sure if genetic engineering was the cause, but there are plenty of ways in which genetic manipulation can boost allergies.

- A gene from a Brazil nut inserted into soybeans made the soy allergenic to those who normally react to Brazil nuts.

- GM soy currently consumed in the US contains a gene from bacteria. The inserted gene creates a protein that was never before part of the human food supply, and might be allergenic.

- Sections of that protein are identical to those found in shrimp and dust mite allergens. According to criteria recommended by the World Health Organization (WHO), this fact should have disqualified GM soy from approval.

- The sequence of the gene that was inserted into soy has inexplicably rearranged over time. The protein it creates is likely to be different than the one intended, and was never subject to any safety studies. It may be allergenic or toxic.

- The process of inserting the foreign gene damaged a section of the soy's own DNA, scrambling its genetic code. This mutation might interfere with DNA expression or create a new, potentially dangerous protein.

- The most common allergen in soy is called trypsin inhibitor. GM soy contains significantly more of this compared with natural soy.

The only human feeding study ever conducted showed that the gene inserted into soybeans spontaneously transferred out of food and into the DNA of gut bacteria. This has several serious implications. First, it means that the bacteria inside our intestines, newly equipped with this foreign gene, may create the novel protein inside of us. If it is allergenic or toxic, it may affect us for the long term, even if we give up eating GM soy.

The same study verified that the promoter, which scientists attach to the inserted gene to permanently switch it on, also transferred to gut bacteria. Research on this promoter suggests that it might unintentionally switch on other genes in the DNA allergens, toxins, carcinogens, or antinutrients. Scientists also theorize that the promoter might switch on dormant viruses embedded in the DNA or generate mutations.

Unfortunately, gene transfer from GM food might not be limited to our gut bacteria. Preliminary results show that the promoter also transferred into rat organs, after they were fed only a single GM meal.

What May Go Wrong

This is only a partial list of what may go wrong with a single GM food crop. The list for others may be longer. Take, for example, the corn inserted with a gene that creates its own pesticide. We eat that pesticide, and plenty of evidence suggests that it is not as benign as the biotech proponents would have us believe. Preliminary evidence, for example, shows that thirty-nine Philippinos living next to a pesticide-producing cornfield developed skin, intestinal, and respiratory reactions while the corn was pollinating. Tests of their blood also showed an immune response to the pesticide. Consider what might happen if the gene that produces the pesticide were to transfer from the corn we eat into our gut bacteria. It could theoretically transform our intestinal flora into living pesticide factories.

GM corn and most GM crops are also injected with antibiotic resistant genes. The ICMR, along with the American Medical Association, the WHO, and organizations worldwide, have expressed concern about the possibility that these might transfer to pathogenic bacteria inside our gut. They are afraid that it might create new, antibiotic resistant super-diseases. The defense that the biotech industry used to counter these fears was that the DNA was fully destroyed during digestion and therefore no such transfer of genes was possible. The human feeding study described above, published in February 2004, overturned this baseless assumption.

No Monitoring

No one monitors human health impacts of GM foods. If the foods were creating health problems in the US population, it might take years or decades before we identified the cause. One epidemic in the 1980's provides a chilling example. A new disease was caused by a brand of the food supplement L-tryptophan, which had been created through genetic modification and contained tiny traces of contaminants. The disease killed about 100 Americans and caused sickness or disability in about 5–10,000 others. The only reason that doctors were able to identify that an epidemic was occurring, was because the disease had three simultaneous characteristics: it was rare, acute, and fast acting. Even then it was nearly missed entirely.

Studies show that the more people learn about GM foods, the less they trust them. In Europe, Japan, and other regions, the press has been far more open about the potential dangers of genetic manipulation. Consequently, consumers there demand that their food supply be GM-free and manufacturers comply. But in the US, most people believe they have never eaten a GM food in their lives (even though they consume them daily). Lacking awareness, complacent consumers have been the key asset for the biotech industry in the US. As a result, millions of Americans are exposed to the potential dangers, and children are most at risk. Perhaps the revelations in the reports released on opposite sides of the planet will awaken consumers as well as regulators, and GM foods on the market will be withdrawn.

The Impact of Genetically Modified Trees on Forests Is Unpredictable

Karen Charman

Karen Charman is a New York–based investigative journalist specializing in agriculture, the environment, and health. In the following selection she discusses the potential impact of genetically modified trees on forests. As she points out, it is impossible to know in advance what this impact will be. Genetically modified trees could spread their genes and alter the genomes of wild trees in ways that cannot be predicted. Also, she states, trees modified for drought or pest resistance might be able to crowd out native vegetation. However, genetically modified trees grown in plantations could help meet world demand for wood products and could offset carbon emissions that contribute to global warming. The key question, Charman says, is what should be done to protect wild forests and who should decide.

At the turn of the last century, nearly one out of every four trees in the eastern deciduous forests of the United States was an American chestnut. Averaging 30 meters tall and 2 meters wide, these majestic beauties ranged from Maine down through the Appalachian mountains and west to Michigan. The fast-growing and naturally rot-resistant chestnut was an important part of early American life, its timber widely used for log cabins, posts, and railroad ties and its abundant nut crop sustaining wildlife as well as livestock.

But within 40 years, a fungal blight had spread throughout the tree's range, felling virtually every chestnut it touched— some 3.5 billion in all. Brought in by a New York nurseryman on imported Asian chestnut seedlings that were then sent all over the country, the blight moved stealthily from tree to tree, entering through a break in the bark and producing an acid that lowered the tree's pH to toxic levels. Because it attacks new shoots before they can mature, the fungus has reduced the once dominant chestnut to little more than a short-lived shrub.

Ever since chestnut blight was first described at the Bronx Zoo in 1904, scientists have been struggling to defeat it. One of several efforts is going on in the labs of Chuck Maynard and Bill Powell, directors of New York State's American Chestnut Research and Restoration Project. The two scientists have been working since the late 1980s to genetically engineer a blight-resistant American chestnut. In the fall of 2004, they made a major breakthrough: shoots finally appeared on a handful of blight-resistant chestnut embryos in petri dishes in Maynard's lab. Each of the tiny embryos had a gene from wheat to give it an extra enzyme, oxalate oxidase, which neutralizes the oxalic acid produced by the blight.

Genetically engineering the chestnut (or any other plant) involves not only inserting foreign DNA into its cells but getting the altered, or "transformed," cells to regenerate into a whole plant. This is particularly difficult with chestnut, because unlike species such as poplar, it won't regenerate from leaf tissue. So Maynard and Powell had to work with immature embryo tissue, which is much more difficult. Unlike the natural transformation a tree seed undergoes in the forest, the method plant biotechnologists use—somatic embryogenesis—is a multi-step, highly sterile, precision operation. It demands vigilant monitoring, special chemical solutions, and filtering equipment to prevent contamination of the fledgling embryos and coax them into seedlings that can survive outside the lab.

Barring unforeseen problems, Maynard and Powell hope to have potted plants by summer 2006, to begin field tests in either the fall or spring, and then to do three years of field trials. If all goes smoothly, they expect to begin deploying genetically modified (GM) American chestnut seedlings to forests in the United States in about four years. Because their goal is to reestablish this tree in its natural range, the two scientists want the Animal and Plant Health Inspection Service (APHIS), the branch of the U.S. agriculture department that regulates biotech plants, to allow their transgenic chestnut genes to spread as far and mix with as many chestnut stump sprouts as possible. In fact, they propose that transgenes from any GM tree in a forest restoration or disease eradication project be granted such regulatory freedom. (In addition to the chestnut, they've engineered transgenic elm seedlings to fight Dutch elm disease, field tested GM hybrid poplars, and identified other pathogens that affect butternut, white pine, beech, dogwood, and oak.)

Impact of Transgenic Trees on Forests Cannot Be Predicted

But it's impossible to know in advance what kind of impacts transgenic trees will have on wild forests. Maynard and Powell see only a minuscule risk of ecological disruption (if any) with their GM chestnut, since it will contain just three or four foreign genes—the target trait plus a few others needed for the desired transformation. The scientists say greater unknowns exist with the conventionally bred and backcrossed American chestnut, which draws one-sixteenth of its genes from its naturally blight-resistant relative, the Chinese chestnut.

Others, however, aren't convinced that ecological safety depends merely on how many foreign genes a transgenic organism contains, particularly when GM organisms may include genes that didn't evolve together and have never existed in nature. Faith Thompson Campbell, a former advocate with American Lands who is now at The Nature Conservancy, summarized the views of many skeptics in her 2000 report "Genetically Engineered Trees: Questions Without Answers." Here, she warns that GM trees planted near large populations of wild relatives will inevitably spread their genes and alter the genomes (the full complement of an organism's genetic material) of wild trees, including those in national parks, wilderness areas, and other reserves. Since the introduced genes have not evolved with those of wild trees, they could have unpredicted impacts and be unstable over the long lifespan of a tree. Moreover, trees modified to exhibit desired traits such as drought or pest resistance may be able to outcompete native vegetation and spread as weeds in wild forests. As a result, Thompson Campbell argues, changing the genetic codes of some trees could have significant impacts on the ecological functioning of an entire forest.

At the same time, large gaps in scientific understanding of forest ecosystems make it difficult to predict, or even recognize, the wider impact of engineered trees. Two leading proponents of GM trees reaffirmed this at a biotech tree conference in North Carolina in November 2004. After describing the monumental effort of sequencing the genes in the Nisqually poplar, Jerry Tuskan, a senior scientist at the Department of Energy's Oak Ridge National Laboratory, said, "So I stand here looking at the poplar genome data set and realize we know nothing about how trees grow." Later, on a panel discussing current knowledge gaps, Ron Sederoff, co-director of the Forest Biotechnology Group at North Carolina State University—and one of the most outspoken advocates for GM trees—admitted, "We don't know a few important things. . . . We don't know what a genome really is. . . . We don't know how many genes there are, because we don't know what a gene really is. We don't know the extent of something that I call epigenomics—the non-genetic changes that occur in genomes that are unstable."

Plant pathologist Doug Gurian-Sherman, a former scientist with the U.S. Environmental Protection Agency who now works at the International Center for Technology Assessment, explains some of the complexities. He notes that trees, and plants in general, produce an array of compounds whose primary purpose appears to be warding off pathogens and harmful insects. This occurs through a sophisticated system of biochemical and metabolic pathways—functions that aren't fully understood by plant physiologists who specialize in the subject, let alone by the molecular biologists manipulating tree DNA. "As biologists, we have to be a little humble and say 'Look, these are complex interactions,'" Gurian-Sherman says. "Frankly, we can't predict how they're all going to play out."

Like many, Gurian-Sherman sees the appeal of wanting to restore the dominant tree in eastern forests. He says there's even a reasonable chance that Maynard and Powell's transgenic chestnuts won't cause harm in the wild because the target trait—the enzyme that neutralizes oxalic acid—is not as obviously disruptive as, say, inserting an insecticide like Bacillus thuringiensis (Bt), which could kill large numbers of nontarget insects. But the only way to really know GM chestnuts won't cause harm, he notes, is to study in a controlled setting how different forest animals, birds, insects, and microorganisms respond over several generations of the tree's lifetime. Different growth cycles in the tree, environmental and climatic changes, and numerous other factors could trigger unintended impacts over time. Avoiding such mistakes is important because, once released, it won't be possible to recall the GM chestnut trees back to the lab.

So far, however, there's no indication that federal regulators will require the GM chestnut to undergo the kind of full environmental risk assessment Gurian-Sherman is calling for, and he's concerned this will set a dangerous precedent. He also predicts the biotech industry will use the example of the transgenic chestnut to say that all genetically engineered trees are safe. "But different transgenes will have very different impacts," he says. "It's like doing a crash test with a Volvo that passed with flying colors. That tells you nothing about how a little Kia will perform in the same test."

Gurian-Sherman's suspicions appear well placed. At the North Carolina biotech meeting in November [2005], forest industry veteran Scott Wallinger, who recently retired from paper giant MeadWestvaco, was one of many speakers who acknowledged the public relations value of the blight-resistant GM chestnut: "This pathway can begin to provide the public with a much more personal sense of the value of forest biotechnology and receptivity to other aspects of genetic engineering."

A Skinhead Earth?

Like their colleagues in agriculture, proponents of forestry biotech use the rationale of looming scarcity and environmental preservation to argue their cause. In a 2000 *Foreign Affairs* article widely quoted in forestry circles, David Victor and Jesse Ausubel offer two visions for the future. In one, "quaint and inefficient agriculture and forestry" lead to a "Skinhead Earth" scenario, where the planet's forest cover shrinks by 200 million hectares by 2050, and lumberjacks regularly shave 40 percent of what remains. Alternatively, "efficient farmers and foresters" who grow "more food and fiber in ever-smaller areas" herald a "Great Restoration" that adds 200 million hectares of forest by 2050 and requires cutting only 12 percent of the world's woodlands to meet global demand for forest products.

Genetically engineered trees grown in intensively managed plantations, or "fast forests," fit into the latter scenario. Today, forest plantations produce one quarter of the world's industrial wood. Though still a tiny percentage of the Earth's nearly 4 billion hectares of forests, they are expanding rapidly, especially in Asia and South America. . . .

Scientists are testing genetically engineered trees with several ... traits of interest to forestry companies, including faster growth, tolerance to drought and salty environments, herbicide resistance, insect resistance (primarily Bt), and altered flowering. More complicated—and more financially risky—traits include straighter-grained and knotless pines, and cold-tolerant eucalyptus trees for plantations in the United States and other places too cold for eucalypts. One of the stranger visions comes from University of Washington molecular biologist Toby Bradshaw, a leading proponent of transgenic trees, who told *Science* in 2002 that trees could one day be "rearchitected" to be, basically, big stumps of wood—"short, wide, almost branchless organisms without extensive root systems" that could pack super-intensive tree plantations.

Experience with GM crops—from Bt corn to Roundup Ready canola—has proven that transgenes spread widely in the environment. But key differences between annual agricultural crops and forest trees make the risks of transgenic contamination in forests even greater. Because of the size of trees, the amount of seeds and pollen they produce, and the updrafts that occur in forests and tree plantations, the scale of gene flow among trees is "unprecedented" compared to food crops, says Claire Williams, a forest geneticist at Duke University. And while most annual agricultural crops cannot survive outside the comparatively simple ecosystem of a farm field, long-lived trees are designed to exist in complex, but poorly understood, wild environments.

Tom Whitham, an ecologist at Northern Arizona University, works with other scientists to document how certain genetic traits affect relationships between trees, understory plants, insects, animals, and micro-organisms. His research shows that genes in individual organisms and populations have "extended phenotypes"—identifiable effects on an ecosystem beyond the organism. Extended phenotypes are particularly important when they occur in dominant plants and keystone species like trees, he says, because they can affect as many as a thousand other species. In addition, traits that may be beneficial under one set of circumstances can become problematic under another. For example, in ongoing research of pinyon pine ecology, Whitham's team discovered that some of the trees are naturally resistant to the stem-boring moth, an insect that eats away at the woody stems. In the first 19 years of their study, the insect-resistant trees did much better. But in a record drought in the twentieth year, about 70 percent of the insect-resistant trees died, while 80 percent of the non-resistant trees survived. "That was a real shock," he says.

In a survey of hundreds of published studies, Whitham found that the more factors a study considered, the greater the likelihood of observing such "ecosystem reversals." He says this is important because changes (including those likely to be induced by genetic engineering) that ignore interactions over time, space, and numbers of species run a high risk of having the opposite effect from what was intended.

Tree biotechnologists acknowledge that GM trees could threaten native forests. But they believe they can solve the problem by making the seeds and pollen sterile, so they cannot reproduce and spread transgenic traits. Yet there is no guarantee a transgenic tree will remain sterile throughout its life. Moreover, many trees, like the American chestnut, also reproduce by sending suckers up from their roots or by regrowing from broken twigs.

Future Prospects

So far, GM trees have not been released commercially, except in China, where more than one million Bt poplars are reported to have been planted nationwide. The reforestation is part of the Chinese government's plan to cover 44 million hectares with trees by 2012 to prevent flooding, droughts, and the spread of deserts. Meanwhile, hundreds of field trials have taken place in the open environment—mostly in the United

States, but also in Canada, Europe, New Zealand, Japan, and a handful of other countries—though researchers in most places are currently required to cut down any GM trees before they flower

Despite their enthusiasm, tree biotechnologists face some challenges before transgenic trees march across the American landscape. The large investments required over long periods are a tough sell in a world where time is money. (Forestry veteran Scott Wallinger laments that the first biotech tree products from 20 years ago are still being tested.) Changing trends in timberland ownership are adding further uncertainty. Investment companies are buying up large tracts of land from forestry corporations, and their commitment to the technology, or even how long they'll own the land, is unknown. After witnessing public resistance to agricultural biotech, GM tree proponents are also very concerned about how the public will react to their plans.

Nevertheless, GM forestry is likely to get a substantial boost from a decision in December 2003 by parties to the UN Framework Convention on Climate Change, the international treaty aimed at reducing emissions of carbon dioxide and other greenhouse gases that contribute to global warming. Under the convention's Kyoto Protocol, which sets specific targets for these reductions, countries will be allowed to offset their carbon emissions by planting tracts of GM trees, which would absorb and store atmospheric carbon. According to Heidi Bachram of the Transnational Institute, millions of dollars in public subsidies are being used as incentives to establish such plantations, despite the questionable benefit of establishing them in lieu of forcing polluters to reduce their emissions up front. Moreover, in order to keep the stored carbon from entering the atmosphere, the plantations would have to be prevented from being burned, destroyed by pests or diseases, or cut down.

Meanwhile, the USDA's [U.S. Department of Agriculture's] APHIS, which oversees field tests and grants permits for the unrestricted commercial release of transgenic plants, is revamping its biotech regulations. In 2003, a National Academy of Sciences study faulted the agency for not having the resources, staff, or expertise to adequately assess the environmental impact of GM releases, especially as the technology progresses. According to Lee Handley, who works for the Risk Assessment Branch of APHIS's Biotechnology Regulatory Services, the agency is considering scrapping the current system of notifications and permits in favor of a new multi-tiered system, where the regulations for a particular GM plant (including both trees and crops) would depend on the environmental risk the agency thought it posed. For example, insect resistant trees might be required to be sterile, while GM trees with other traits might not. APHIS is also considering adding a category of "conditional release" that would require additional data to be collected on a given planting over time. . . .

Final regulations will come out following the agency's review of comments. Handley, a forest industry veteran, has strongly urged industry members to make their voices heard by participating in the public comment period. At the North Carolina conference he warned participants that GM trees "are definitely on the radar screen" of environmental groups, which are "very well organized and sophisticated"—which suggests just how nervous biotech tree proponents are, since most mainstream environmental groups have not addressed this issue, and very few people know genetically engineered trees even exist.

In their *Foreign Affairs* piece, David Victor and Jesse Ausubel remind us that "forests matter": they host much of the planet's biodiversity, protect watersheds and provide clean drinking water, and remove carbon dioxide from the atmosphere. "Forests count—not just for their ecological and industrial services but also for the sake of order and beauty," they write. A key question as we consider genetically engineered forests is what to do to preserve wild forests, and who gets to decide.

Genetically Modified Organisms Can Produce Useful Chemicals

Economist

The Economist *is a major weekly newspaper, published in London but distributed worldwide. Its policy is to publish all articles anonymously. The following selection discusses the use of genetically modified bacteria to produce environmentally friendly chemicals for industrial use. The article explains that this might lead to an economy based on what are now waste materials from plants, instead of on oil and other hydrocarbons. It would then be possible to produce almost limitless supplies of fuels, such as ethanol to replace gasoline, and plastics. Genetically engineered bacteria might even be made to produce hydrogen for use in fuel cells. Still another application of genetic engineering to industry, the article mentions, is the production of spider silk in goats' milk.*

Once upon a time, much of the man-made world consisted of things that had been grown. Clothes, carpets, bedsheets and blankets were woven from wool, flax, cotton or (if you were lucky) silk. Shoes were made of leather. Furniture and fittings were made of wood, which also served as fuel for heating and cooking. Then humanity discovered coal, oil and chemistry. Today only the poorest and the richest people burn wood, and many of its other uses have been taken over by plastics. Natural fibres, too, have ceded much of the market to artificial ones. But biology may be about to revenge itself on the synthetic, petroleum-based industrial world by providing new materials and fuels. And in this guise, it may even become acceptable to the environmental movement.

In truth, biotechnology has been quietly working away at industrial applications for some years. It started with enzymes. A business in purifying and selling bacterial enzymes for use in food manufacturing, washing powders and so on has existed for decades, but in 1988 a Danish firm called Novozymes produced the first transgenic enzyme, a fat-digester for detergents. Partly thanks to this lead, Novozymes is now the world's largest enzyme manufacturer, hotly pursued by several other firms.

Enzymes are proteins, which have a reputation for being fussy molecules. Expose them to the wrong temperature, acidity, salinity or pressure and they stop working, sometimes permanently. And the temperature, acidity, salinity and pressure of industrial chemistry is often very different from that found in familiar living organisms. However, it has become clear that lots of bacteria thrive in conditions that used to be regarded as hostile to life. Quite a cottage industry, known as bioprospecting, has developed to collect these bacteria from hot springs, soda lakes, arctic rocks, industrial-effluent outlets and so on. Enzyme companies then analyse the bugs for proteins that look like useful starting points for the sort of directed evolution used by firms such as Applied Molecular Evolution, Genencor and Maxygen in their search for drugs.

Enzyme-catalysed processes have always been a more efficient way of making molecules than traditional chemistry. They often involve fewer synthetic steps, and the yield of each of those steps is almost always close to 100%, whereas the cumulative losses from step to step of doing things in a complicated traditional synthesis mean that the yield may easily end up below 10%. But until recently, the range of reactions for which enzymes could be used was limited, and their fussiness confined them to high-value products such as drugs and vitamins. Now, thanks to directed evolution, there is serious talk of using enzymes to make cheap, bulk chemicals. And not only talk: action, too.

Genetically Engineered Bacteria Help Produce Plastics and Fuels

The most promising applications for the new model enzymes over the next decade are plastics and fuels. The two most advanced plastics projects are those of DuPont, one of the world's biggest chemical companies, and Cargill-Dow, a joint venture between the agricultural and chemical firms of those names. DuPont's process, developed in collaboration with Genencor, took biochemical pathways from three different microorganisms and assembled them into a single bacterium. The raw material for the process is glucose syrup made from maize starch. This is converted into a molecule called 1,3 propandiol, which is used to make a polyester called Sorona. But Sorona is only half biological. It is a copolymer—that is, it is made out of two sorts of monomers—and the other one, a molecule called terephthalate, still has to be made from oil, so there is some way to go.

Cargill-Dow is closer. Its product, Ingeo, is made out of lactic acid, which in turn is made from glucose. Traditional techniques are used only for the polymerisation of the individual lactic-acid monomers into polylactic acid (the chemical name for Ingeo). The stuff is being made in commercial quantities at a plant in Nebraska, and [went] on the market [in 2003]. At the moment it is rather more expensive than its petrochemical competitors, but Cargill-Dow hopes to brand it as a premium product in the market for environmentally friendly goods.

Biopolymers are environmentally friendly twice over. Since their manufacture uses little in the way of fossil hydrocarbons, they do not add to global warming. And because they are biodegradable, they cause no pollution when discarded. The firms' bigwigs seem hopeful that this will prove a big enough attraction to allow them to reap economies of scale that will then make their products truly cost-competitive.

DuPont and Dow are giants, but biopolymers can be for minnows too. Metabolix, a small firm based in Cambridge, Massachusetts, takes the process for making them to its logical conclusion—by getting living organisms to do the polymerisation as well as making the monomers.

Animals and plants store surplus energy in the form of carbohydrates, oils and fats. Some bacteria, though, use a different molecule, called a polyhydroxyalkanoate, or PHA. About a decade ago, when they were working at the nearby Whitehead Institute, James Barber and Oliver Peoples, the founders of Metabolix, realised that this material might be put to use as a plastic. They have spent the past ten years proving the point.

Having prospected the bacterial world for appropriate enzymes, and assembled enzymatic pathways in the same way that Genencor did for DuPont, they came up with something new: bugs that actually make plastics and store them inside themselves, in large quantities (about 80% of the weight of a grown bacterium is plastic) and in great variety. PHAs are not a single chemical, but a vast molecular family. Different enzyme pathways can turn out different monomers, producing plastics with different properties. Indeed, it is possible to have two different enzyme pathways within the same bacterium. The result is a co-polymer that expands the range of properties still further.

Metabolix, which planned to start commercial production [in 2003], has shown that its PHAs, too, can be produced at a price which is competitive with at least the more expensive existing polymers, such as polyesters. That in itself may not be enough to convince manufacturers to switch from tried and trusted materials to Metabolix's novel ones, but the firm hopes that in the large market for single-use items the added feature of biodegradability will be a clincher. If manufacturers do not make the change unprompted, then a nudge from the regulators might be expected. Currently, plastic is a persistent form of rubbish, whereas an object made of PHA will disappear in a few weeks if dumped in a landfill, or even in the sea.

Get the price right, then, and the opportunities are enormous. According to a report published in 2001 by McKinsey, a consultancy, by 2010 biotechnology will be a competitive way of producing about a fifth of the world's chemical output by value. That means white [industrial] biotech will be competing in a market worth $280 billion, of which McKinsey thinks the technology might capture about $160 billion. As biotech processes become cheaper, those numbers will increase.

All the companies working in this field have projects designed to bring down the costs. Metabolix, for example, hopes to switch from growing plastics in bacteria (which have to be fed) to growing them in plants (which will make them out of water, carbon dioxide and sunlight). The firm's researchers have already shown that this is possible in the laboratory. They are now scaling up the process.

Waste Materials from Plants Might Be Made Useful

The enzyme firms, meanwhile, are working on an idea that would allow whole plants to be used as chemical feedstock. Glucose syrup is a refined product, made from maize grains, which form only a small part of the plant. Maize grains cost about $80 a tonne. That is cheaper than petroleum, weight for weight, but the researchers think they can improve on this. Instead of the grains, which are the most valuable part of the plant, they are trying to find ways of using the waste, which fetches only about $30 a tonne for silage. Unfortunately, it consists mainly of cellulose, a natural polymer of glucose but a recalcitrant one.

Help, though, is at hand. The reason dead plants do not stay around indefinitely is that they are eaten by bacteria.

These bacteria contain cellulose-digesting enzymes known as cellulases. Genencor and several of its rivals are using this as the starting point for building a better cellulase. Verdia, Maxygen's plant-biotechnology subsidiary, is hoping to go one better. Its researchers are working on developing a cellulase that the plant would make in its own cell walls. To prevent the enzyme digesting the living plant, it would be tweaked to work most effectively in conditions found not inside plants but in bioreactors.

If these ideas come off, then an era of limitless supplies of glucose could follow. That would allow the production not only of as much plastic as anyone could want, but also of another product that can easily be made from glucose: ethanol. This is not only the active ingredient of booze, but also an efficient fuel. Henry Ford's first car was powered by it. Today, some of the motor fuel sold in Brazil is pure ethanol, which modern engines can be tuned to run on happily, and the rest is 20% ethanol. Even in the United States nearly a tenth of all motor fuel sold is a blend of 90% petrol and 10% ethanol. And since the carbon in ethanol made from plants came out of the atmosphere, putting it back there cannot possibly cause any global warming.

At this point some people in the industry turn starry-eyed and start talking about a future "carbohydrate economy" that might replace the existing "hydrocarbon economy". The countryside would be rejuvenated as a source of raw materials. Land now taken out of cultivation would be put back to use. Small-scale chemical plants to process the stuff would pop up everywhere. And the oil-producing countries would find themselves out of a job.

Surprisingly, these visionaries are often hard-headed businessmen. Even more surprisingly, the numbers they are bandying do not sound all that exotic. The American market for bioethanol is already 8 billion litres a year. The enthusiasts at Genencor reckon it could be as high as 75 billion litres a year by 2020. That would be enough to replace two-thirds of America's current petrol production. In January, a Canadian firm called Iogen opened a small cellulase-powered pilot plant that converts straw into ethanol.

Finding enzymes such as cellulases involves, as mentioned earlier, bioprospecting. But there is bioprospecting, and then there is Craig Venter. Dr Venter was the man behind Celera, the company that took on the Human Genome Consortium. The firm got its scientific edge from a technique called whole-genome shotgun sequencing, which he had developed to work out the genetic sequences of bacteria in one go. Using the money Celera had raised, Dr Venter applied the technique to the much more complicated task of working out the human genome in one go. Now, he proposes to apply it to entire eco-systems, working out the genomes of all the critters in them by a similar, one-step approach. Admittedly the critters are bacteria, and the ecosystems are water samples from the Sargasso Sea. But such samples will have thousands of species in them, most of which cannot be cultured in the laboratory and are therefore inaccessible to standard sequencing methods.

Whole-genome shotgunning works by shredding the DNA of an organism into tiny pieces, sequencing the pieces, then sticking the results together again in the right order, using a powerful computer and clever software. Whole-ecosystem shotgunning aims to do the same with all the DNA in a sample, regardless of how many species it comes from. If the software is good enough, it will be able to sort the pieces into the individual genomes.

Genetic Engineering Might Be Used to Produce Energy

Dr Venter is full of ideas about what might be done with his discoveries, even before he has made them. But he is particularly excited by the possibilities for energy generation, and recently set up a new organisation, the Institute for Biological

Energy Alternatives, to investigate them further. In his view, replacing petrol [gasoline] with ethanol is old-think. New-think would power the world not with internal combustion engines but with fuel cells. And fuel cells use hydrogen.

One way to make hydrogen biotechnologically might be with a bug called Carboxydothermus, which was discovered in a hydrothermal vent (an undersea volcanic spring) off the coast of Russia. This species lives by reacting carbon monoxide with water. One of the waste products is hydrogen. A more promising route might be to intercept the hydrogen ions produced in the first step of photosynthesis. Another of Dr Venter's pet projects, creating a bacterium with a completely synthetic genome, could come into its own here. By leaving out the genes for the sugar-forming pathways that normally use these hydrogen ions, such a creature could be made to devote all its energies to producing hydrogen. Nor could it escape into the outside world (always a worry with bio-engineered bugs), because it would lack the biochemical apparatus to survive there. Thus trapped, it could, he muses, be used in solar-powered fuel cells for such applications as portable computers.

That points to the power of industrial biotechnology to create completely new products. The idea of a partly living fuel cell may be merely dipping a toe in the ocean of possibilities. Another dipped toe is that of Nexia Biotechnologies, based in Quebec, which is using technology similar to that of GTC Biotherapeutics to turn out spider silk in goats' milk. Spiders, observes Jeffrey Turner, the firm's boss, have been perfecting silk for the past 400 years. Such silk comes in many varieties, which do different jobs for spiders and can thus do different jobs for people. For Nexia's products, these jobs range from stopping bullets when the silk is worn as body armour to stitching up eyeballs after surgery.

Some firms, such as Genencor, are starting to explore wilder shores. As proponents of nanotechnology (the incipient field of building devices a few billionths of a metre across) are wont to observe, biology is natural nanotechnology. Why, then, go to all the trouble of creating an artificial nanotechnology from scratch? Genencor is collaborating with Dow Corning, a big materials company, in this area. Among other things, the firms are looking at rhodopsins, the protein molecules that act as light-detecting pigments in a range of organisms from bacteria to people. Genencor has bred 21 rhodopsin-type molecules, each of which responds to a particular wavelength of light. These molecules might have applications as switches in photonics, the as yet largely hypothetical idea that data could be processed by light instead of by electronics. These are small-scale investments, and may come to nothing, but they are worth a flutter.

However, there are shores yet wilder than these awaiting, where big battles are almost guaranteed. For among the prospects offered by biotechnology is one hitherto reserved for science fiction: tailor-made humans.

Genetically Engineered Organisms Can Help to Clean Up Pollution

John C. Avise

John C. Avise is a professor of genetics at the University of Georgia. In the following selection he discusses how genetically modified organisms may be used to clean up environmental pollution. As he explains, scientists hope to engineer plants that can draw up mercury or other poisons through their roots, thus removing it from contaminated soil. Some plants, such as poplar trees, naturally do this with certain pollutants, and it may become possible to enhance the process or transfer it to faster-growing plants. Some bacteria can detect and even degrade explosives, and someday their genes may be inserted into plants to help decontaminate munitions storage sites. Other uses for genetic engineering in getting rid of pollution explained by Avise include the restoration of farmland and the cleanup of oil spills.

Biotechnologists are keen to do more than biomonitor for pollutants; they also want to clean up the environment. There is plenty to be done. The Environmental Protection Agency [EPA] estimates that at least 30,000 polluted sites in the United States are in need of remediation from toxic wastes. In the United Kingdom, 100,000 contaminated sites are known or suspected, affecting about 1% of its total land area. These and untold numbers of other sites around the world are polluted with witches' brews of routine organic and inorganic compounds, an unhappy legacy of decades of industry, mining, unwise agricultural practices, and other human activities.

Various heavy metals that have been released into soils or waterways are particularly troublesome for several reasons.

John C. Avise, *The Hope, Hype and Reality of Genetic Engineering: Remarkable Stories from Agriculture, Industry, Medicine, and the Environment.* New York: Oxford University Press, 2004. Copyright © 2004 by Oxford University Press, Inc. Reproduced by permission.

First, when transferred at high doses to living tissue, they can be teratogenic (i.e., induce developmental malformations) in fetuses, as well as toxic or carcinogenic (cancer-causing) at any life stage. Second, unlike many organic compounds, heavy metals cannot be broken down into nontoxic subunits (although some can be modified into less harmful forms). Finally, heavy metal residues are widespread in the environment, originating from such diverse sources as leaded paints and gasolines, scrap metals, expended ammunition, power plant wastes, and industrial chemicals (leaked, discarded, or abandoned).

Cleaning Up Mercury

The dangers of heavy metals as well as the opportunities they present for bioremediation are well illustrated by mercury (Hg). This toxic element enters the environment either in volatile liquid form [metallic Hg(o)] typically from industrial accidents, or in nonvolatile particulate form [ionic Hg(II)] in dregs from trash, burnt coal, or commercial chemicals (as well as from natural volcanic activity). Any form of mercury can be toxic, but the most serious problems usually come from methylmercury (MeHg), a compound naturally produced by anaerobic bacteria when their habitats are polluted by metallic or ionic mercury. Methylmercury is a potent toxin because, as it moves up food webs into flesh-eating animals (including humans), it becomes bio-concentrated by several orders of magnitude.

The world was alerted to the danger of methylmercury by a disaster on Japan's Kyushu Island in the 1950s. For years, a chemical factory had dumped wastewater laden with mercury into Minamata Bay, resulting in the death of many shellfish, fish, and birds. Nobody paid much heed, however, until cats began to convulse and die in droves, and local villagers experienced an epidemic of sensory disturbances and brain lesions. . . .

How might biotechnology help clean up mercury spills? Researchers at the University of Georgia think they have an answer in transgenic plants engineered to detoxify mercury's more poisonous forms. Experimental mustard plants were modified to carry two genes of bacterial origin: *merA*, which converts Hg(II) to Hg(o), and *merB*, which degrades MeHg to methane and Hg(II). Hg(o) is a relatively benign form of mercury [100-fold less toxic than Hg(II)] that the GM [genetically modified] plants either sequester in their tissues or volatilize into the atmosphere as they transpire water vapor through surface pores. Due to their newly acquired metal-detoxification systems, these transgenic plants can withstand levels of soil mercury about 10–50 times greater than those that kill non-GM controls.

Of course, the intent is not to produce mercury-resistant plants per se, but rather to enlist GM plants to cleanse contaminated soils or waters. The idea is that appropriate transgenic plants will draw up MeHg or Hg(II) through their roots, process these poisons to Hg(o), and release the elemental mercury harmlessly into the air. Whether this approach will work on large outdoor scales required for environmental restoration remains to be demonstrated, but the promise appears great.

Many Environmental Pollutants Might Be Eliminated

Mercury is just one of many environmental pollutants projected for ecological cleanup using GM plants. Cadmium, cesium, chromium, lead, selenium, strontium, tritium, and uranium are other poisonous waste-site elements that engineered plants someday might help decontaminate. So, too, is arsenic, which contaminates drinking water in Bangladesh and parts of India and causes health problems for an estimated 110 million people. Recently, researchers moved arsenic-processing genes (that absorb and bind arsenic from soils) from bacteria into experimental plants. The hope is that such GM plants can be mass planted in arsenic-contaminated areas to help sequester this environmental poison. . . .

Phytoremediation (environmental restoration by plants) could provide an ecologically friendly alternative to current pollution cleanup methods. Once in operation, the process would be sun-powered and potentially low in cost (relative to conventional remediation techniques such as soil excavation and removal). Phytoremediation also has some limits, however: It is slower than soil excavation, it can clean soil only to the depth of the GM plants' roots, and there is still the problem of how to harvest and dispose of the metal toxins sequestered in the GM plants' tissues. Other concerns are that the metal-sequestering transgenes might escape (via hybridization) into wild or cultivated relatives of the engineered plants, and that the toxin-laden plants might be eaten by wildlife, either harming the herbivores directly or by harming other species up the food chain.

In a broader sense, phytoremediation, promoted by humans, is nothing new. For centuries, farmers have rotated crops with leguminous plants to fertilize nitrogen-depleted soils, foresters have seeded barren landscapes to control erosion, and gardeners have planted aquatic vegetation to oxygenate and filter polluted waters. From this perspective, genetic engineering is just a new-age way to enlist plants to modify environments for human purposes.

Phytoremediation of Organic Pollutants

Many plants come naturally well suited as environmental monitors and cleansers. Their root surfaces often are extensive and chemically sensitive, having evolved specifically to adsorb (accumulate on the outside) or absorb (take inside) nutrients from soils and waters. Most plants have innate systems for translocating, sequestering, and sometimes deporting (e.g., via transpiration or leaf fall) toxic foreign compounds. Plants col-

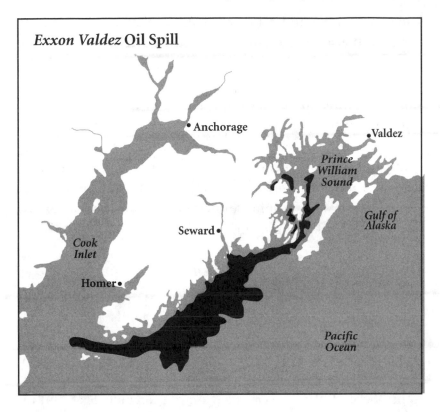

Exxon Valdez Oil Spill

lectively have huge biomass, making them potentially useful as repositories and/or detoxifiers for vast amounts of pollutants. Plants in effect are "self-powering" systems, equipped with solar panels (leaves) that collect energy from natural sunlight. Finally, being sedentary and dependent on local environmental conditions, many plants have evolved genetic capabilities to detoxify or otherwise ameliorate the poisonous effects of numerous site-specific contaminants.

By genetically tweaking plants for improved adsorption, uptake, transport, storage, degradation, or volatilization of environmental toxins, biotechnologists are now attempting to upgrade plants' natural proclivities for bioremediation. . . .

Trichloroethylene (TCE), a toxic and carcinogenic industrial solvent, is a widely distributed pollutant of groundwaters and soils. Native plants grown at polluted sites long have been known to extract and transpire (emit as a vapor) TCE and to promote the growth of root-associated bacteria that degrade the compound. A more recent discovery is that poplar trees, *Populus*, also produce enzymes that break apart TCE into simple chlorine compounds and harmless carbon dioxide. As more is learned about the mechanistic details and the taxonomic distribution of this degradative pathway, it may become possible for genetic engineers to enhance the trees' own detoxification processes or to transfer them into other plant species perhaps more suitable for remediation efforts (e.g., by virtue of being faster growing).

Decontaminating Sites of Stored Munitions

A second research example is somewhat farther along. . . . Some bacteria can detect explosive compounds such as TNT, and genetic engineers have built upon this native ability by fusing reporter transgenes to the bacterial sensor genes such that the microbes fluoresce when grown in contact with landmines. Several plant species likewise can degrade TNT and related explosive compounds such as nitroglycerin, albeit at modest efficiencies. Recently, a nitroreductase gene was isolated from bacterial colonies and inserted into tobacco plants. These transgenic seedlings tolerate TNT and nitroglycerin far better than do non-transgenic controls and apparently break down nitroglycerin at about double the normal pace. This gives a substantial boost to prospects that plantations of transgenic plants may someday help decontaminate the thousands of acres of polluted land and rivers near sites that produce, store, and dispose of munitions.

A third example involves PCBs [polychlorinated biphenyls], among the world's worst pollutants due to their acute biotoxicity, wide distribution, and long half-life in the environment. Some plants degrade PCBs with modest effectiveness, as do various bacterial species that collectively have dozens of genes for this task. Using recombinant DNA techniques, biotechnologists hope to wed various microbial and plant genes, insert the genetic constructs back into plants, and sow those GM strains that offer the best prospects for phytoremo diation of PCB-contaminated lands. . . .

In nearly every bioremediation project involving GM plants, questions of the following sort will arise. Can any toxic compounds accumulated in plants' tissues be harvested and disposed of safely (if they are not already detoxified by the plants themselves)? Might the transgenes escape from the site of release, or transfer to other species, and with what consequences? Might some of the transgenic plants themselves disrupt the ecological communities they enter? There may be risks, but the health and well-being of humans and natural ecosystems already have been compromised by the toxins and pollutants that we have spewed into the environment. Thus, another ultimately compelling question for society will arise as well: Do we have any rational choice but to act?

Farmland Restoration

Another form of environmental remediation is farmland restoration. Since the 1940s, unwise farming practices around the world have led to a substantial reduction in the plant-growing capacity of an acreage roughly equal to China plus India and the almost hopeless ruination of an area the size of Hungary. To return such land to productivity could go a long way toward alleviating world hunger without jeopardizing wild lands not yet cultivated.

Much of this farmland degradation is due to salt accumulation in soils. When crops are irrigated over the years with mineral-laden water, continued evaporation can lead to the deposition of calcium and magnesium salts that are toxic to most plants. . . .

Soil erosion is another major problem. Every year, globally, plowed farmlands lose an estimated 25 billion metric tons of topsoil to wind and water. Some of the most dramatic episodes are associated with periodic drought. For example, throughout the 1930s, a large mid-section of the U.S. southern interior, formerly a wheat-growing region, became a desolate dust bowl from a combination of dry conditions, overgrazing, and overplowing. Winds whipped across the desiccated fields, raising billowing dust clouds that carried away the precious topsoil, blackened the skies for days, and resulted in a mass exodus of thousands of farm families from the barren land.

Through plant genetic engineering, some scientists think that they can help societies avoid such disasters, as well as reclaim farmland that already is degraded. . . .

One suggested approach is to engineer salt-tolerant plants, and at least one such example already exists. In 2001, reports appeared concerning the construction of GM tomato plants that can grow in highly saline soils. Scientists engineered this feat by implanting regular tomato plants with a transgene encoding a membrane transport protein hooked up to a promoter sequence from a virus. In the GM plant, this genetic construct proved to pump salt ions from the soil, via roots and tissues, into cellular storage sacks known as vacuoles. The GM tomato plants were able to grow in soils nearly one-third as briny as seawater and 50 times saltier than their non-GM brethren can tolerate. Salt accumulated in the leaves, so the fruit reportedly tasted normal. If such GM plants can be commercialized, they promise not only to make salt-polluted acreage more productive, but also to rehabilitate such farmland to its original, functional low-salt condition.

Engineering Crops for Drought Tolerance

A related approach showing promise is to engineer crop plants for drought tolerance, both to mitigate chronic water shortages (probably the biggest single threat to world food production) and to ward off singular disasters like the Dust

Bowl. Several genes recently have been identified that naturally help plants cope with arid conditions, as well as with
other stresses such as cold and salinity. Drought damage, salinity injury (which occurs when roots can't extract enough
freshwater from salt-laden soils), and harm from frost (which
occurs when water seeped from cells forms ice crystals in in-
tercellular spaces) are all, in effect, symptoms of plant dehy-
dration. By tinkering with various promoter sequences and
genes and inserting the genetic constructs into cotton, tobacco, tomato, potato, canola, and others, researchers are trying to imbue several major crop species with the ability to tolerate desiccation. The Rockefeller Foundation in New York
recently committed up to $50 million to this effort by sup-
porting a decade-long global effort to improve drought resistance in GM maize and rice, for example.

If successful, such genetic modifications would have obvious benefits, but also some potential environmental dangers
that sometimes get neglected in all the ballyhoo. Crops engineered for greater tolerance to salt, cold, or drought likely
would be planted not only on reclaimed farmland, but also in
areas such as ocean margins and deserts previously deemed
uncultivable. In such cases what constitutes "environmental
remediation" may be in the eye of the beholder. Extensive
wheatlands covering the Mojave Desert, for example, would
not be everyone's idea of an environmental improvement....

Cries over Spilled Oil

Near midnight on March 24, 1989, a huge oil tanker struck
Bligh Reef in Prince William Sound, Alaska, disgorging 11
million gallons of crude oil into pristine waters and intertidal
zones. The *Exxon Valdez* spill sparked a public outcry as sea
otters, birds, and other marine life died gruesome deaths before TV cameras and a beautiful coastline was desecrated by
black toxins. Emergency efforts to mitigate the disaster by
conventional means—mechanical booms and skimmers,

chemicals sprayed to disperse the pollution, and a fire purposefully lit to burn the crude oil—were thwarted by bad weather conditions and the sheer volume of the spill.

The *Exxon Valdez* was the largest maritime oil spill in U.S. history, and it prompted Congress to pass the Oil Pollution Act of 1990 that tightened oil-tanker industry regulations. But in terms of petroleum volumes, the Alaskan catastrophe at that time ranked only 28th on the all-time global list. The largest discharge, in 1979, was a 78-million-gallon spill from the *Atlantic Express* in the West Indies. Other infamous headliners were the 1978 *Amoco Cadiz* disaster along the French coast (68 million gallons), and the 1967 *Torrey Canyon* calamity in the English Channel (38 million gallons).

Other petroleum disasters have started on land. In March 1993, 400,000 gallons of oil spewed from a ruptured pipeline in Fairfax County, Virginia. In January 1988, a 4-million-gallon storage tank split apart in Floreffe, Pennsylvania, sending out a surge of oil that contaminated the Monongahela and then the Ohio rivers, killing wildlife, and for a time debilitating the economic, as well as the environmental, health of the region. As devastating as such local incidents can be, the total volume of oil that all such disasters belch into the environment pales in comparison to the chronic global release of 300-million gallons, annually, from nonaccidental sources such as routine road runoff and vehicle maintenance. Sooner or later, most leaked oil ends up in oceans.

Native soil and water bacteria are able to break down most petroleum products, eventually to carbon dioxide, water, and microbial biomass, but the process is too slow to have significant quick impacts on serious oil spills. To enhance such microbial bioremediation, two traditional approaches are used: fertilization and seeding. The first method, also called nutrient enrichment or biostimulation, involves adding phosphorus, nitrogen, or other substances to foster the growth of microbes capable of oil degradation. The second method, also called bioaugmentation, involves adding nonindigenous bacteria to boost the oil-degrading rate of the resident microbial population at polluted sites. Although both are widely used for U.S. oil spills, neither method is hugely effective in shoreline cleanup, especially on wave-tossed shorelines such as the coast where the *Exxon Valdez* foundered.

Engineering Microbes for Oil Cleanup

Some biotechnologists think they can genetically engineer microbes for improved oil-cleaning performance in nature. Indeed, the first bioremediation field trial for any genetically modified microbe [GMM] involved a bacterium modified to better degrade naphthalene, a petroleum product. The process began with natural strains of *Pseudomonas fluorescens* isolated from soils at a gas-manufacturing plant. In the laboratory, plasmids were constructed and used to transform the parent strain so that it contained genes for naphthalene degradation fused to a bioluminescent reporter gene. The procedure was done in such a way that the GMM emitted bioluminescence in direct proportion to its rate of naphthalene degradation, thereby providing a built-in visible monitor of its performance. When released into contaminated subsurface soils, the GMMs remained viable and gradually did their duty, breaking down naphthalene pollutants.

An additional problem, salinity, attends efforts to engineer bacteria for the degradation of oil and other hydrocarbons in the marine realm. Most known oil-eating bacteria have been isolated from terrestrial environments and thus do poorly or die when exposed to the salty conditions of estuaries and shorelines. So, another group of geneticists recently engineered strains of *Pseudomonas* to contain osmoregulation genes that permit the bacteria to live in hypersaline environments. The strains already possessed a genetic capacity to attack various chemical fractions of crude oil, so the new

GMMs, it is hoped, someday may help clean up oil disasters in and near oceans.

Regardless of any foreseeable success for remediation biotechnology, full restoration from major oil spills will remain a long-term process, and ecological harm will be done in the interim. Thus, even if GMMs someday do prove to be genuinely helpful, it will always be wise to focus primary efforts on preventing such spills in the first place.

Genetic Modification of Insects Involves Benefits and Risks

Aaron Zitner

Aaron Zitner is a staff writer for the Los Angeles Times. *In the following selection he describes scientists' plans to genetically modify insects that destroy crops or cause human disease. As he explains, this could be of immense benefit to agriculture and, even more importantly, in the prevention of diseases that now kill thousands of people. However, there would be risks in doing this because once an insect is released there is no way to control where it flies, and it might mutate over time into something dangerous. Zitner reports the opinions of several researchers on the issue of whether these risks would be acceptable.*

Charles Beard's recipe for stopping the kissing bug, a tropical pest that kills 50,000 people each year, calls for ammonia, ink and guar gum. The result is an odorous goop that resembles the bug dung that, unpleasant as it may seem, happens to be a vital meal for young kissing bugs.

But Beard adds something else to his faux feces that could prove to be even more noxious. It is genetically engineered bacteria that, once ingested, render the kissing bug unable to pass along its deadly disease.

Now, a world that is already debating the safety of gene-spliced foods is about to meet a new class of genetically engineered organisms: modified bugs. Beard's creation is just one in a series of plans to turn insects and bacteria into warriors against disease and crop pests.

[In the] summer [of 2001], scientists hope[d] to start the first U.S. field tests on a gene-spliced insect—a version of a moth that chews through $24 million worth of U.S. cotton plants each year. Researchers are also trying to create mosquitoes that cannot carry malaria, which still kills 1 million a year, or West Nile fever, which is spreading across the United States. On the drawing board are ticks that cannot carry Lyme disease or Rocky Mountain spotted fever. Although the work is advancing quickly, questions remain about which U.S. agencies would monitor the new organisms.

If released in the wild, scientists say, a properly engineered bug would spread its disease-defusing trait to its wild cousins, protecting a whole community or region. Public health officials say the bugs could be a crucial new weapon against often-deadly diseases such as malaria, which has built resistance to drugs and pesticides and has reemerged in places where it was once defeated.

"The situation is awfully bleak out there," said Barry Beaty, an insect specialist at Colorado State University. "A lot of people are dying. We need new ways to respond to the problem."

Ecologists Worry About Genetically Modified Bugs

But if much of the world is anxious about genetically engineered foods, then modified bugs are sure to set off alarms as well. "Once you release an insect, it flies, and you can't control its distribution in the environment," cautioned Svata Louda, a University of Nebraska plant ecologist. "That's just one of the things that makes ecologists apprehensive about new versions of an insect."

Critics also ask whether an engineered bug gene might mutate over time into something dangerous, or whether it would jump to an unintended insect species. Another question: Given that bugs travel freely, how many people in an area would have to give consent before gene-spliced bugs were released?

Scientists say they have kept these questions well in mind over the last decade. But it is only now, thanks to funding from such heavyweights as the U.S. government and the World Health Organization, that they have accomplished enough in the lab to start thinking about conducting field tests that would produce some answers.

In London ..., researchers from around the world [convened in June 2001 to] hash out basic scientific questions about field trials—where they might be conducted, what data should be collected and how they should be monitored. The meeting is sponsored by the WHO [World Health Organization], the National Institutes of Health [NIH] and London's Imperial College.

At the same time, U.S. officials say they are taking some early, tentative steps to sort out which agency should make sure that the new bugs pose no harm to people or the environment.

In some cases, jurisdiction seems clear. In July [2001], for example, scientists from the U.S. Department of Agriculture [USDA] and UC Riverside hope[d] to start the first field test of a gene-spliced insect, the pink bollworm moth, a bane to cotton growers. Because the Agriculture Department itself has authority over plant pests, it has claimed jurisdiction over the field trial. [The trial was still on hold as of 2005.]

The scientists want to place 2,350 gene-altered moths in a large mesh cage in an Arizona cotton field. Their long-term plan is to insert a lethal gene into the moth that would be passed to their offspring, wiping out the next generation of insects. But in their first field trial, the scientists will use only a marker gene and watch how it affects moth behavior.

Robert Rose, a USDA official charged with assessing the scientists' plan, said he is considering the stability of the mesh cage and the fitness of altered moths to survive in the wild. Only sterile moths would be put into the cage, he said, a step that aims to diminish their effect on the environment if they escape.

Federal jurisdiction is less clear over other bugs now being developed. A "talking points" document by the NIH says "there are gaps" in the existing law covering field tests.

An antimalaria mosquito, for example, would not be considered a plant pest and therefore would probably not fall under USDA jurisdiction, Rose said. But officials at the Environmental Protection Agency say it is not clear that they would oversee the mosquitoes, either.

The Plan to Eradicate the Kissing Bug

Beard, a parasitic-disease specialist with the Centers for Disease Control and Prevention [CDC], says he consulted the CDC's own biosafety committee about his plans for the kissing bug. The bug has infected 14 million people in Central and South America with Chagas disease, which causes heart and digestive problems that kill 50,000 a year.

Kissing bugs hide in the thatch huts common in the developing world, and they feed on the blood of people and animals. But the bugs cannot live on blood alone. They must also consume bacteria, Rhodococcus rhodnii, which they pick up from the dung of their parents.

Beard has produced a gene-altered version of the bacteria and loaded it into his fake dung. Once the bug eats the dung, the bacteria attack and kill any Chagas disease agent that the bug is also carrying.

"We've tested this concept in jars. Now we want to test it in a place that's more like the field," Beard said recently near his CDC office outside Atlanta.

He swept open the door to a greenhouse to show his plan. Inside, he had built a protective mesh tent, and then a second mesh tent inside the first. Within that, he had built a small thatch hut, the kind that might be found in Honduras or Guatemala. . . .

Beard and his research partner, Dr. Ravi Durvasula of Yale University, plan to seed the hut with the fake dung, then release a handful of kissing bugs. They want to study how the altered bacteria flow through the kissing bug population. Like the moth researchers, Beard is using bacteria that carry only a marker gene, not the gene designed to attack Chagas disease. The tents are meant to stop the kissing bugs from escaping.

Agriculture officials in California also have high hopes for gene-altered insects, as they continue the battle against the Mediterranean fruit fly.

State and federal officials control the crop-eating pest by flooding the environment with sterile males, which crowd out wild males in the competition for females and yet produce no offspring. Officials release about 500 million sterile flies each week in Southern California, at an annual cost of $15.8 million. A similar program in Florida costs nearly $3 million.

To sterilize the flies, officials use radiation, which also leaves the insects weak and diminishes their ability to mate in the wild. Researchers think they would have a more robust fly if they accomplished the sterilization through a genetic flaw. "If we could release, say, 75,000 flies per square mile instead of 250,000, that would save money," said Patrick Minyard, an official with the state Agriculture Department.

Views of Risk Change over Time

Several researchers said bug scientists should take heed of the past problems with introducing new insects to the environment.

A fly released in 1906 and for decades afterward to control the gypsy moth has also caused damage to 200 other butterflies and moths in the Northeast, said Jeff Boettner, an insect specialist at the University of Massachusetts in Amherst. The fly's wide appetite was known at the time, but researchers believed that was a good trait.

Now, they want to preserve many of the targeted butterflies. "We change our views over time about what risk is and what is proper," Boettner said.

Louda, the Nebraska researcher, said weevils released in the state to control an invasive, foreign thistle plant have also attacked a native thistle more than expected. This suggests that the present tools are "not sufficient" for evaluating what effect a new insect species will have on plants, she said.

But Rebecca Goldburg of Environmental Defense, which questions the safety of bioengineered foods, suggested that people might find a certain amount of risk acceptable if it helped stop disease.

"People have been more reluctant to take on environmental risk when we see the benefit of a product going to big biotech and chemical companies," she said. "Consumers in general are less concerned if sick people are getting the benefit."

CHAPTER 2

Genetic Engineering
in Medicine

Human Organs May Be Grown in Genetically Modified Animals

Sylvia Pagán Westphal

Sylvia Pagán Westphal is a science journalist with a background in biology. In the following selection she describes the work scientists are doing in xenotransplantation, which is the implantation of cells from one species into another. As she states, in the future it may become possible to grow tissues or even whole organs in animals and give them to people who need transplants. This would allow doctors to obtain cells compatible with the patient's immune system without having to create human embryos through therapeutic cloning, which would get around the ethical objections some people have to the medical use of human embryos. However, Westphal says, there are people who oppose the creation of any human-animal chimeras (organisms containing cells from more than one species). Also, some worry that combining human cells with animals might cause viruses in animal DNA to mutate into forms that could infect people.

It's bad news, says your doctor. Your liver is failing. So he extracts stem cells from your bone marrow and injects them into a sheep fetus while it is still in the womb. When the sheep is born, much of the animal's liver will consist of your own cells—ready to be harvested and given back to you.

This dream therapy is still years off, if it happens at all, but the first steps have already been taken by a team led by Esmail Zanjani at the University of Nevada, Reno. "Esmail has some pretty startling results," says Alan Flake of the Children's Hospital of Philadelphia.

Zanjani's team hopes the animal-human chimeras they are creating will one day yield new cells genetically identical to a patient's own for repairing damaged organs, and perhaps larger pieces for transplantation.

It might even be possible to transfer whole organs, since in some cases having at least a partly human organ would be better than a purely animal xenotransplant [a transplant between two species]. Immune rejection of the animal portion would still be a problem, but it is not insurmountable, says Flake. "I don't think that in 10 to 15 years that's out of the question."

Advantages of Growing Human Cells in Animals

If perfected, the technique could overcome some of the big stumbling blocks facing researchers who want to make tissues and organs for implants. It might yield significant quantities of just about any kind of cell or tissue, for instance, with no need to fiddle about with different culture conditions or growth factors.

Instead, the host animal's own developmental program guides the injected human stem cells into their final roles. "We take advantage of the growing nature of the fetus," Zanjani says.

It would also allow doctors to obtain immune-compatible cells without having to create human embryos by therapeutic cloning. Human cells could be separated from the animal ones simply by modifying existing cell-sorting machines.

Providing the method really does produce normal human cells, they would not be rejected. And any stray animal cells would be killed off by the recipient's immune system.

Of course, the idea of using part-human, part-animal chimeras as living factories for producing cells or organs raises a host of ethical and safety issues. There is the risk of transferring animal diseases to humans, for a start. And the creation of such chimeras has long been controversial. Is a sheep with human cells making up part of its brain no longer just a sheep?

Injecting Human Cells into Sheep

Zanjani's original goal was to see if unborn children with genetic defects could be treated by injecting healthy stem cells into the fetus. This is still his main aim, but while doing animal experiments he realised the technique could also be used to grow "humanised" organs.

The first hint this might work came from work done by Flake a few years ago. He showed that when human mesenchymal stem cells extracted from bone marrow are injected into sheep fetuses, the human cells become part of the heart, skin, muscle, fat and other tissues. But the numbers of human cells were very low. Zanjani's team has now managed to produce sheep-human chimeras with a surprisingly high proportion of human cells in some organs. According to results presented at a conference . . . in December [2003], in some cases between seven and 15 per cent of all the cells in the sheep's livers are human.

The human cells must be injected around halfway through gestation—before the fetus's immune system has learned the difference between its own and foreign cells, so that the animal does not reject them, but after the body plan has formed.

That ensures that the resulting animals look like normal sheep rather than strange hybrids like the "geep", created by fusing the embryos of a sheep and goat.

In some cases the human liver cells cluster together to form functional, fully human liver units, says Graca Almeida-Porada of the Nevada team. These units could be transplanted whole as auxiliary organs, says Zanjani.

What is more, human albumin—a blood protein produced by the liver—has been detected in the host animals' blood. The work has been submitted for publication.

Growing Heart Cells May Become Possible

Meanwhile, results of similar experiments on the heart will be published early in 2004. "The type of stem cells we use make a lot of heart cells," is all Zanjani will say about these experiments.

If he is right, it would be an important advance because it would open the door to creating fetal heart cells for therapy. For example, a kind of fetal heart cell called a cardiomyocyte has been shown to be especially good at repairing hearts in rats or mice, but there is one big obstacle: at the moment the only source of human fetal heart cells is human fetuses.

Robert Kloner, a heart expert at the University of Southern California in Los Angeles, says an approach like Zanjani's would get around this ethical issue.

Zanjani says it might also be possible to grow a wide range of other tissues, such as insulin-producing islet cells for treating diabetes. And he hopes it will be possible to increase the proportion of human cells in organs still further.

The team is now trying to identify subpopulations of stem cells that might be better at producing one organ or another. Their results also hint that the timing and site of the injection make a difference.

But all members of the Nevada team stress that the technique is years, if not decades away from being tested in humans. For starters, it will be crucial to make sure the human cells really are functional. Recent experiments have suggested that some stem cells fuse with other cells when injected, rather than forming normal heart cells or liver cells.

A key question is whether the human cells fuse with sheep cells, says Philip Noguchi, head of the Center for Biologics Evaluation and Research at the US Food and Drug Administration. It would not necessarily be the death knell if the cells do fuse, but it would be important to know what problems it presents, Noguchi says.

Zanjani is optimistic, however: with human cells making up such a large proportion of some chimera organs, he thinks the sheep would die if these cells were dysfunctional fused cells.

Opposition to Xenotransplantation

All the same, there is widespread opposition to xenotransplantation in countries such as the UK and Canada. One big worry is that retroviruses lurking in animal DNA could mutate into forms that infect people.

The US is more open to the idea, and a few clinical trials are under way, but health concerns mean Zanjani's technique would be expensive to develop.

What is more, companies are unlikely to invest in the method because he has not tried to patent it. And it could even be unpatentable: in 1998, the US Patent Office declared it unlikely that it would grant any more patents on part-human inventions.

Then there is the moral issue. Some people oppose the creation of all human-animal chimeras on religious grounds, and many more would join them if there were the slightest chance that sheep with human brain cells might be more than just sheep.

Zanjani doesn't rule out the possibility entirely. "There is no way for us to know," he says. "But at the level we're working with the animal, it's still a sheep."

The Ethical Concerns of Adding Human Cells to Genetically Modified Animals

Maryann Mott

Maryann Mott is a freelance writer who lives in Arizona and specializes in writing about animals. In the following selection she discusses the troubling questions that are raised by the creation of chimeras, hybrid creatures that are part animal and part human. She explains that scientists are experimenting with the creation of genetically modified animals that contain human cells, both for research purposes and with the hope of future medical uses such as the growing of human organs in animals for transplant. However, as she says, some people believe that it is wrong to cross animals with humans. Canada has passed a law against putting human cells into animal embryos; some think this should be banned in the United States also, while others believe such a ban would stop research that could save human lives.

Scientists have begun blurring the line between human and animal by producing chimeras—a hybrid creature that's part human, part animal.

Chinese scientists at the Shanghai Second Medical University in 2003 successfully fused human cells with rabbit eggs. The embryos were reportedly the first human-animal chimeras successfully created. They were allowed to develop for several days in a laboratory dish before the scientists destroyed the embryos to harvest their stem cells.

In Minnesota last year [2004] researchers at the Mayo Clinic created pigs with human blood flowing through their bodies.

And at Stanford University in California an experiment [is planned] to create mice with human [brain cells].

Scientists feel that, the more humanlike the animal, the better research model it makes for testing drugs or possibly growing "spare parts," such as livers, to transplant into humans.

Watching how human cells mature and interact in a living creature may also lead to the discoveries of new medical treatments.

But creating human-animal chimeras—named after a monster in Greek mythology that had a lion's head, goat's body, and serpent's tail—has raised troubling questions: What new subhuman combination should be produced and for what purpose? At what point would it be considered human? And what rights, if any, should it have?

There are currently no U.S. federal laws that address these issues.

Ethical Guidelines

The National Academy of Sciences, which advises the U.S. government, has been studying the issue. In March [2005] it plans to present voluntary ethical guidelines for researchers. [The guidelines were released in April 2005.]

A chimera is a mixture of two or more species in one body. Not all are considered troubling, though.

For example, faulty human heart valves are routinely replaced with ones taken from cows and pigs. The surgery which makes the recipient a human-animal chimera—is widely accepted. And for years scientists have added human genes to bacteria and farm animals.

What's caused the uproar is the mixing of human stem cells with embryonic animals to create new species.

Biotechnology activist Jeremy Rifkin is opposed to crossing species boundaries, because he believes animals have the right to exist without being tampered with or crossed with another species.

He concedes that these studies would lead to some medical breakthroughs. Still, they should not be done.

"There are other ways to advance medicine and human health besides going out into the strange, brave new world of chimeric animals," Rifkin said, adding that sophisticated computer models can substitute for experimentation on live animals.

"One doesn't have to be religious or into animal rights to think this doesn't make sense," he continued. "It's the scientists who want to do this. They've now gone over the edge into the pathological domain."

David Magnus, director of the Stanford Center for Biomedical Ethics at Stanford University, believes the real worry is whether or not chimeras will be put to uses that are problematic, risky, or dangerous.

Human Born to Mice Parents?

For example, an experiment that would raise concerns, he said, is genetically engineering mice to produce human sperm and eggs, then doing in vitro fertilization to produce a child whose parents are a pair of mice.

"Most people would find that problematic," Magnus said, "but those uses are bizarre and not, to the best of my knowledge, anything that anybody is remotely contemplating. Most uses of chimeras are actually much more relevant to practical concerns."

Canada recently passed the Assisted Human Reproduction Act, which bans chimeras. Specifically, it prohibits transferring a nonhuman cell into a human embryo and putting human cells into a nonhuman embryo.

Cynthia Cohen is a member of Canada's Stem Cell Oversight Committee, which oversees research protocols to ensure they are in accordance with the new guidelines.

She believes a ban should also be put into place in the U.S.

Creating chimeras, she said, by mixing human and animal gametes (sperms and eggs) or transferring reproductive cells, diminishes human dignity.

"It would deny that there is something distinctive and valuable about human beings that ought to be honored and protected," said Cohen, who is also the senior research fellow at Georgetown University's Kennedy Institute of Ethics in Washington, D.C.

But, she noted, the wording on such a ban needs to be developed carefully. It shouldn't outlaw ethical and legitimate experiments—such as transferring a limited number of adult human stem cells into animal embryos in order to learn how they proliferate and grow during the prenatal period.

Irv Weissman, director of Stanford University's Institute of Cancer/Stem Cell Biology and Medicine in California, is against a ban in the United States.

"Anybody who puts their own moral guidance in the way of this biomedical science, where they want to impose their will—not just be part of an argument—if that leads to a ban or moratorium . . . they are stopping research that would save human lives," he said.

Mice with Human Brain Cells

Weissman has already created mice with brains that [contain] about one percent human [cells]. . . . He may conduct another experiment where the mice have 100 percent human [brain neurons]. This would be done, he said, by injecting human neurons into the brains of embryonic mice.

Before being born, the mice would be killed and dissected to see if the architecture of a human brain had formed. If it did, he'd look for traces of human cognitive behavior.

Weissman said he's not a mad scientist trying to create a human in an animal body. He hopes the experiment leads to a better understanding of how the brain works, which would be useful in treating diseases like Alzheimer's or Parkinson's disease.

The test has not yet begun. Weissman is waiting [for the scientific community's approval].

William Cheshire, associate professor of neurology at the Mayo Clinic's Jacksonville, Florida, branch, feels that combining human and animal neurons is problematic.

"This is unexplored biologic territory," he said. "Whatever moral threshold of human neural development we might choose to set as the limit for such an experiment, there would be a considerable risk of exceeding that limit before it could be recognized."

Cheshire supports research that combines human and animal cells to study cellular function. As an undergraduate he participated in research that fused human and mouse cells.

But where he draws the ethical line is on research that would destroy a human embryo to obtain cells, or research that would create an organism that is partly human and partly animal.

"We must be cautious not to violate the integrity of humanity or of animal life over which we have a stewardship responsibility," said Cheshire, a member of Christian Medical and Dental Associations. "Research projects that create human-animal chimeras risk disturbing fragile ecosystems, endanger health, and affront species integrity."

Gene Therapy Will Revolutionize the Practice of Medicine

Michael Fumento

Michael Fumento is an author, journalist, and attorney special-
izing in science and health issues. He is the author of five books.
In the following excerpt from his book BioEvolution *he describes*
ways in which experimental gene therapy is being used to treat
disease. He states that gene therapy not only holds great promise
for treating hereditary diseases but may be able to cure other ill-
nesses such as cancer, heart disease, and blindness. The major
problem is finding ways to deliver the therapeutic genes, that is,
to insert them into the body, but scientists are working to do
this. As Fumento points out, it will be some time before gene
therapy can be used on a large scale because it has not yet been
governmentally approved. However, individuals involved in clini-
cal trials have already benefited from such therapy.

"Twenty years from now gene therapy will have revolutionized the practice of medicine," predicted Dr. W. French
Anderson in 1999. Anderson is director of gene therapy at the
Keck School of Medicine at the University of Southern California in Los Angeles, and the most prominent pioneer in the
field. "Virtually every disease will have gene therapy as one of
its treatments." But that is what people were saying ten years
earlier with almost nothing to show for it. Now gene therapy
is the "comeback kid" of biotech with over six hundred clinical trials involving almost 3,500 patients by late 2002.

All of the early gene therapy experiments took advantage
of the infectious power of viruses, which by nature burrow

into the nucleus of living creatures and set up housekeeping there. Viruses comprise a tiny section of DNA or RNA stuffed inside a protein envelope. Researchers render the virus benign by deleting the harmful gene or genes; then they splice the therapeutic gene into the remaining genetic material and mix it with human cells. The altered virus, called a carrier or a vector, can deliver the therapeutic gene into the nucleus.

The first real breakthrough in gene therapy came in April 2000, involving two infants born with a life-threatening illness called "severe combined immunodeficiency disorder" that had forced them to live inside protective sterile "bubbles." French researchers first removed millions of stem cells from each infant's marrow. (Stem cells are those that haven't yet matured into a final cell type. . . .) Then the researchers employed genetically altered viruses to deliver to those cells healthy copies of the gene the children lacked, and reinfused the altered cells into the children. Over two years later they reported that the children were still healthy and that they had successfully treated another two chilren as well. In June 2002 came the announcement that two more children were apparently cured of the disease through gene therapy. In a truly international effort, Italian and Israeli researchers treated a Colombian child and a child from an Arab community in Israel. "We've known it ought to work, and fortunately it did," said W. French Anderson. "This tells us that if you can get a high enough percentage of cells fixed, gene therapy will cure you."

Gene therapy holds great promise for correcting hereditary disorders. . . . Originally, the purpose of gene therapy was to do precisely what the French researchers did: treat a disease caused by a single defective gene by replacing it with a good one. Then scientists made a discovery that changed all that: they found that adding genes that caused the right proteins to be produced could potentially alleviate any number of disorders.

Gene Therapy for Cancer

At virtually the same time the world heard about the "bubble boy" successes, the *Wall Street Journal* reported the case of a woman with terminal lung cancer who had a new gene inserted to replace the defective one, the p53, that had allowed the tumor to form and grow. After insertion of the new gene, her tumor "shrank into a little ball and surgeons handily removed it." In a male patient, the *Journal* reported, treatment appeared to have wiped out a tumor the size of a large lemon. Genetic therapy involving repair of p53 is now in advanced human trials for head and neck cancer, ovarian cancer and lung cancer in combination with radiation. In fact, while most people still equate gene therapy with fixing hereditary problems that strike children, almost two-thirds of clinical trials are now directed against cancer.

Some results have been simply stunning. "Malignant glioma (a cancer of the brain) is almost always fatal, due to very poor response to surgery, radiation and chemotherapy," declared Matthias Gromeier of Duke University at the annual meeting of the American Society for Microbiology in May of 2001. But, he went on to say, "We have developed a new form of therapy against malignant glioma based on viruses that can cause brain infections in humans."

The virus is essentially the same one that causes crippling and often fatal poliomyelitis. But Gromeier's team tamed it by inserting a small piece of genetic material from a cold virus into the poliovirus genome, effectively rendering it "completely unable" to cause polio in healthy neuronal cells. They injected the hybrid virus into mice with malignant gliomas and found that tumors were "eliminated by the replicating virus within days," and none of the mice contracted polio. . . .

Delivering the Genes

"There are only three problems in gene therapy," according to Inder Verma, a professor at the Salk Institute for Biological

Studies in La Jolla, California. "Delivery, delivery, and delivery. It isn't going to be a problem to make gene therapy work—if we have an appropriate set of tools to deliver the genes."

The need for better gene delivery, however, is leading to the development of some ingenious techniques. University of Pittsburgh scientists have trimmed a gene down to size to be able to insert it. . . . It codes for a dystrophin protein that holds great promise for curing sufferers of Duchenne muscular dystrophy, an inherited disease for which there is no real treatment and which cripples and eventually kills about one in 3,500 males. The protein vexed researchers because it's 640 times larger than the virus into which it would have to be inserted to be useful as gene therapy. So Dr. Xiao Xiao and his colleagues at Pitt essentially stripped away any part of the gene that didn't appear vital to its function. The result was three different "mini-genes," all of which were inserted into the virus and then injected into the calf muscles of mice lacking natural dystrophin protein. Two of the slimmed-down genes stimulated the manufacture of the protein in 90 percent of treated tissue. Dystrophin continued to be pumped out for at least a year—the duration of the experiments.

Another way of inserting larger genes employs bacteria rather than viruses. Virginia Waters of the University of California, San Diego, has found that bacteria can "have sex" with mammalian cells. The bacteria she used had been genetically engineered to contain pieces of DNA called plasmids. These readily transfer between two bacteria and are actually a vital tool in crop biotechnology. But mammalian cells aren't known to accept bacterial DNA. Perhaps it was just something that occurred rarely and had never been observed.

To find out, Waters inserted a gene into one of the plasmids that would show up under a special light. She then laid the bacteria on top of a layer of mammalian cells, and after eight hours used the light to determine that the desired hanky-panky had indeed transpired. This "bacterial conjugation," as

"Bubble Baby" Gene Therapy

In gene therapy treatment of severe combined immunodeficiency disorder, stem cells are first extracted from an afflicted infant's marrow. A genetically modified virus is then used to carry into the cells the gene the baby lacks. The resulting enhanced stem cells are reinfused into the infant. The stem cells reintegrate with the infant's system to supply to it the previously missing gene, which produces the desired recuperative results.

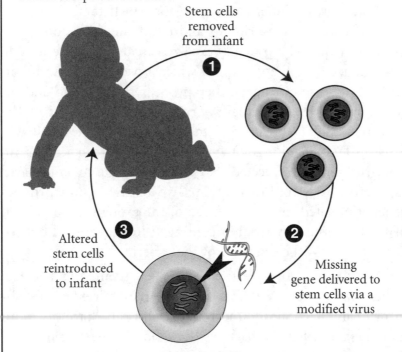

Stem cells removed from infant

①

③
Altered stem cells reintroduced to infant

②
Missing gene delivered to stem cells via a modified virus

she described it, could conceivably deliver even the largest genes to a variety of sites in humans.

The Danger of Using Viruses

Unfortunately, size isn't the only problem with viral vectors. Viruses can have immunological side effects. In 1999, the first known death clearly attributable to gene therapy occurred at the University of Pennsylvania's Institute for Human Gene

Therapy. Eighteen-year-old Jesse Gelsinger, who'd had a gene that had been engineered into a weakened adenovirus (a cold virus) injected into his liver to treat a rare metabolic disorder, subsequently died of a severe immune reaction. The tragedy was that Gelsinger's disorder was not fatal. His death prompted the Food and Drug Administration [FDA] to suspend all human gene therapy trials at the institute. It appears that Gelsinger died from proteins on the surface of the coat of the virus, which had not been removed. But the possibility of harm from using viruses was not lost on the medical community. This concern was reinforced three years later when a three-year-old "bubble boy" was diagnosed with a disease very similar to leukemia, followed by another such child in early 2003. Both children had been part of experiments to build their immune systems using retroviruses, which researchers had long thought in exceptional cases could cause cancer if they lodged in or near a cancer-causing gene. That appears to be what happened with both children. But hundreds of humans and far more lab animals had been given such viruses without harm. Indeed, the researchers who originally treated the boys had success with nine out of eleven, so one could make the utilitarian argument that the children were given a treatable albeit *possibly* terminal disease in place of a *certainly* lethal one. Nonetheless, "do no harm" demanded that related types of research be suspended, putting an even higher premium on funding nonviral vectors. . . .

Bringing New Life to Older Blood Vessels

Gene therapy also holds tremendous promise for treating heart disease by replacing or strengthening blood vessels. Dr. Keith Channon of Oxford University and his colleagues are using modified viruses to put new DNA into veins, making them stronger. "It has great potential as this is an extremely large problem in modern medicine. It could save lives and improve outcomes from surgery," Channon said. Others have successfully used synthetic blood vessels, but these tend to clog up and cause dangerous blood clots, especially when they are thin and implanted in parts of the body where blood flow is sluggish.

If you have clogged arteries, you may get to bypass coronary bypass surgery with angioplasty, a medical procedure in which a doctor inserts a small tube (a catheter) with a balloon on the end into the affected artery. The doctor will inflate the balloon after it is placed in the narrowed area, stretching out the artery and improving blood flow. But how can you keep the artery from constricting again after the balloon is deflated and removed? One way is with stents, tiny metallic scaffolds that are a miniaturized version of the way tunnelers keep the walls and ceiling in place while they dig further. But the metaphor ends there, because usually your body reacts to the little scaffolds as intruders, and cells soon repopulate and block the artery. That's what happened to Vice President Dick Cheney in February of 2001, when doctors discovered that an artery into which they had inserted a stent just three months earlier was already 90 percent blocked. Doctors at Children's Hospital of Philadelphia, however, may have found a way around this problem, by coating the stents with genetic material that would inhibit cell production. Dr. Robert Levy and his team, using live pigs, found that about 1 percent of the cells from the walls of coronary arteries that had received stents coated with the polymer-DNA mixture expressed the gene within a week. More than that, gene expression was largely restricted to the coronary arteries, spreading only slightly to other organs. Levy said gene-therapy stents could be used in humans [in the near future].

Gene Therapy for Blindness

The video showed a scene that was a bit bizarre and perhaps seemingly cruel. Three dogs were walking around a room, occasionally bumping into objects. Curiously, though, they bumped into objects on one side only. That's because this breed of dogs, Briards, though congenitally blind because of long-term breeding that went awry, could now see out of one eye treated with gene therapy. The dogs had functional genes injected into their eyes piggybacked aboard a harmless adenovirus. About ten thousand Americans now alive were born with essentially the same disease the dogs had, Leber's congenital amaurosis (LCA). Children with LCA are born with little or no vision, and whatever they may have at birth they lose. The illness is one of several incurable forms of blindness collectively known as retinitis pigmentosa, which afflicts more than 100,000 Americans by destroying specific nerve cells in the retina. To sufferers of LCA, these dogs represent hope for the miracle of sight.

This study, led by researchers at the University of Pennsylvania, marked the first time that congenital blindness has been cured in anything larger than a mouse. But "exactly the same approach could be used with humans," said lead researcher Dr. Jean Bennett. "The protocol we used to deliver the therapeutic reagent [to the Briards] is exactly the same that is used every day by retinal surgeons to remove fluid under the retina, [and to] remove abnormally growing cells."

The scientists first gave the dogs injections into their left eyes but in an area far from the retina. As expected, this had no effect. But into the right eyes, they injected corrected genes directly behind the retina, very close to the retinal pigment epithelial cells. The videos along with electrical measurements of the retina and measured pupil responses, clearly showed that the animals had attained a relatively high degree of vision. "We have to be careful not to fill people with false expectations or false hopes," said Albert Maguire, an ophthalmologist at the University of Pennsylvania's Scheie Eye Institute who wasn't involved in the study. "But that said, it's hard not to get very excited about this, because it's a very dramatic result. I mean, basically these dogs were blind and now they are not blind anymore."

The Pennsylvania researchers believe that similar gene therapy treatments may prove to be a cure for as many as 150,000 Americans suffering from retinal diseases. Further, if the gene therapy works in LCA patients, it could be the vanguard for treating a broad array of hereditary vision diseases that strike the retina. "It should open the floodgates," said Dr. Gerald Chader, chief scientific officer of the Foundation Fighting Blindness in Owings Mills, Maryland.

Treating Hemophilia with Genes

In 2000, kids at Children's Hospital in Philadelphia with hemophilia B were successfully treated with genes that helped their bodies make a blood-clotting protein they lacked, called factor IX. About five thousand Americans suffer from hemophilia B, a hereditary disease in which the body produces insufficient levels of this protein. As a result, blood leaks into their joints. Treatment for the disease involves injections of purified factor IX, which itself is now bioengineered. Traditional transfusion treatment improves symptoms but is no cure. Many patients are disabled by age thirty, and some still die of complications.

The new gene's effect was "modest, but measurable," said Mark Kay, the study leader and a member of the Department of Genetics at the Stanford University School of Medicine. "It changes from severe disease to moderate, which really increases the quality of life for the individual." . . .

Using Genes to Treat Tremors

It's estimated that about 1.5 million Americans suffer from [Parkinson's disease, a] progressive neurodegenerative disorder. While it's rarely fatal, it can be terribly incapacitating. Symptoms include tremors, slowness of movement, stiffness of limbs, and problems with gait or balance. It's generally a disease of older persons, but as actor Michael J. Fox's struggle with Parkinson's reminds us, that is not always the case. Although no one knows what causes the disease, it involves a gradual loss of neurons in one region of the brain. These neurons specialize in producing the signaling chemical dopamine, and as dopamine production declines there is a gradual loss of muscular control. There are various treatments for the symptoms, the major ones designed to add dopamine back in. One that seemed promising over a decade ago was called glial-derived neurotrophic factor (GDNF), but doctors tried repeatedly to inject it directly into the brain, without success. Until recently, that is. A gene therapy study in late 2000 was "able to completely reverse the changes" that lead to Parkinson's symptoms in aged Rhesus monkeys. In young monkeys given a Parkinson's-like disease, "We halted the disease process, and in fact reversed it," said neuroscientist Jeffrey Kordower of Rush Presbyterian—St. Luke's Medical Center in Chicago.

Looking ahead, many gene therapists think the next big advance will be a mechanism in the vector that won't just implant a gene but will regulate it as well. "Most diseases and most drugs require modifying the dose," explained James Wilson, director of the Institute for Human Gene Therapy at the University of Pennsylvania. "But the genes carried into cells by currently used vectors are either on or off." Wilson said the mechanism he envisions "will be like a genetic rheostat. The gene will not work until you take a pill, and the more pills you take, the more the gene will be expressed—and if you want to cut off the supply, you simply stop taking the pill."

Don't expect any widespread applications of gene therapy [by 2008]. (Even putting a drug on the so-called "fast track" usually speeds up the process by perhaps only six months to a year.) Individuals in trials will continue to benefit, with some completely cured but there are just too many kinks to be worked out now for broader use. When official approvals come, however, they will bring sweeping changes, as they already have to a lucky few in clinics.

Gene Therapy May Not Be Beneficial to Society

Jeremy Rifkin

Jeremy Rifkin is president of the Foundation on Economic Trends, a private foundation based in Washington, D.C. He is the author of many books and articles and is a prominent opponent of bio-technology. In the following selection he explains the difference between somatic gene therapy, in which the changes made to an individual's genes are not passed on to offspring, and germ line gene therapy, in which such changes affect future generations. He states that so far, the results of somatic gene therapy have been disappointing, although its supporters continue to believe that it will prove successful in treating genetic disorders. Germ line gene therapy, as he points out, is much more controversial; it has many advantages, but on the other hand, if it becomes common, people will find it hard to draw a line between merely correcting serious defects and conferring desired genetic qualities. A parent's failure to have an unborn child's gene corrected might come to be regarded as a crime. Moreover, the question of what should be considered a "defect" will be troubling. In Rifkin's opinion, in-stead of attempting to design future generations through gene therapy, it might be better to use knowledge about the human genome to analyze the relationship between disease and environ-mental factors.

While the 20th century was shaped largely by spectacular breakthroughs in the fields of physics and chemistry, the 21st century will belong to the biological sciences. Scientists around the world are quickly deciphering the genetic code of life, unlocking the mystery of millions of years of biological evolution on Earth. Global life science companies, in turn, are beginning to exploit the new advances in biology in a myriad of ways, laying the economic framework for the coming Biotech Century.

Genes are the raw resource of the new economic epoch and are already being used in a variety of international business fields—including agriculture, animal husbandry, energy, bioremediation, building and packing materials, and pharmaceuticals—to fashion a bio-industrial world. Nowhere is the new genetic commerce likely to have a bigger impact, however, than in human medicine. For the first time in history, the scientific tools are becoming available to manipulate the genetic instructions in human cells. Human gene therapy raises the very real possibility that we might be able to engineer the genetic blueprints of our own species and begin to redirect the future course of our biological evolution on Earth. Breakthroughs in genetic technology are bringing us to the edge of a new eugenics era with untold consequences for present and future generations and for civilization itself.

In less than ten years, the global life science companies will hold patents on many of the 30,000 or so genes that make up the human race as well as patents on the cell lines, tissues, and organs of our species, giving them unprecedented power to dictate the terms by which we and future generations live our lives. The concentration of power in the global pharmaceutical industry has already reached staggering proportions. The implications of a new market-driven eugenics are enormous and far reaching. Indeed, commercial eugenics could become the defining social dynamic of the new century.

Friendly Eugenics

The term "eugenics" was conceived by Sir Francis Galton, Charles Darwin's cousin, in the 19th century and is generally divided along two lines. Negative eugenics involves the systematic elimination of so-called biologically undesirable traits. Positive eugenics is concerned with the use of genetic manipulation to "improve" the characteristics of an organism or species.

The prospect of creating a new eugenic man and woman is becoming ever more likely as a result of the steady advances in somatic and germ line genetic engineering technology. In somatic therapy, intervention takes place only within somatic cells and the genetic changes do not transfer into the offspring. In germ line therapy, genetic changes are made in the sperm, egg, or embryonic cells, and are passed along to future generations. Somatic gene surgery has been carried out in limited human clinical trials for more than a decade. Germ line experiments have been successfully carried out on mammals for more than 15 years and researchers expect the first human trials to be conducted in the near future.

Despite years of favorable media reports on various somatic gene therapy experiments and the high expectations voiced by the medical establishment and the biotech industry, the results have, thus far, been disappointing. So disappointing, in fact, that the National Institutes of Health (NIH) itself was forced to acknowledge the results and issue a sober warning to scientists conducting the experiments to stop making promises that could not be kept. After surveying all 106 clinical gene therapy trials conducted over a five-year period, involving more than 597 patients, a panel of experts convened by the NIH reported that "clinical efficacy has not been definitively demonstrated at this time in any gene therapy protocol, despite anecdotal claims of successful therapy." Still, many of the staunchest supporters of the new gene therapies remain convinced that the techniques will bear fruit as methodologies and procedures are refined and new knowledge of the workings of genes become more available to researchers and clinicians.

Debate over Germ Line Therapy

Far more controversial is the prospect of conducting human germ line therapy. Programming genetic changes into the human germ line to direct the evolutionary development of future generations may be the most radical human experiment ever contemplated and raises unprecedented moral, social, and environmental risks for the whole of humanity. Consequently, debate over genetic manipulation of human eggs, sperm, and embryonic cells has raged for more than 20 years.

Even so, a growing number of molecular biologists, medical practitioners, and pharmaceutical companies are anxious to take the gamble, convinced that controlling our evolutionary destiny is humankind's next great social frontier. Their arguments are couched in terms of personal health, individual choice, and collective responsibility for future generations.

Writing in *The Journal of Medicine and Philosophy*, Dr. Burke Zimmerman makes several points in defense of germ line cell therapy over somatic cell therapy. To begin with, he argues that the increasing use of somatic therapy is only likely to increase the number of survivors with defective genes in their germ lines, who will pass an increasing number of genetic problems onto succeeding generations. Second, although this therapy may be able to treat many global disorders by replacing populations of cells, it may never prove effective in addressing diseases involving solid tissues, organs, and functions dependent on structure, like, for example, the brain, making germ line therapy the only likely solution to such disorders.

Proponents of germ line therapy argue for broadening the ethical mandate of the global health profession to include responsibility for the health of those not yet conceived. The interests of the patient, says Zimmerman, should be extended to include the interests of "the entire genetic legacy that may result from intervention in the germ line." Moreover, parents ought not to be denied their right as parents to make choices on how best to protect the health of their unborn children during pregnancy. Therefore, it is argued that to deny parents the opportunity to take corrective action in the germ line would be a serious breach of medical responsibility.

Finally, the health costs to global society need to be factored into the equation, say the advocates of germ line therapy. Although the costs of genetic intervention into the germ line to cure diseases will likely remain high in the early years, the cost should drop dramatically as the methods and techniques become more refined. The lifetime cost of caring for generations of patients suffering from Parkinson's disease or severe Down's syndrome is likely to be far greater than simple prevention in the form of genetic intervention at the germ line level.

Genetic Responsibility

In the coming decades, scientists will learn more about how genes function. They will become increasingly adept at turning genes "on" and "off." They will become more sophisticated in the techniques of recombining genes and altering genetic codes. At every step of the way, conscious decisions will have to be made as to which kinds of permanent changes in the biological codes of life are worth pursuing and which are not. A global society steeped in "engineering" the gene pool of the planet cannot possibly hope to escape the kind of on-going eugenics decisions that go hand-in-hand with each new advance in biotechnology. There will be enormous social pressure to conform with the underlying logic of genetic engineering, especially when it comes to its human applications.

Parents in the biotech century will be increasingly forced to decide whether to take their chances with the traditional genetic lottery and use their own unaltered egg and sperm, knowing their children may inherit some "undesirable" traits, or undergo corrective gene changes on their sperm, egg, embryo, or fetus, or substitute egg or sperm from a donor through in vitro fertilization and surrogacy arrangements. If they choose to go with the traditional approach and let genetic fate determine their child's biological destiny, they could find themselves culpable if something goes dreadfully wrong in the developing fetus, something they could have avoided had they made use of corrective genetic intervention at the sex cell or embryo stage.

In the biotech century, a parent's failure to correct genetic defects in utero might well be regarded as a heinous crime. Society may conclude that every parent has a responsibility to provide as safe and secure an environment as humanly possible for their unborn child. Not to do so might be considered a breach of parental duty for which the parents could be held morally, if not legally, liable. Mothers have already been held liable for having given birth to cocaine-addicted babies and babies with fetal alcohol syndrome. Prosecutors have argued that mothers passing on these painful addictions to their unborn children are culpable under existing child abuse statutes and ought to be held liable for the effect of their life style on their babies.

Why Stop with Eliminating Defects?

Proponents of human genetic engineering argue that it would be cruel and irresponsible not to use this powerful new technology to eliminate serious "genetic disorders." The problem with this argument, says the *New York Times* in an editorial entitled, "Whether to Make Perfect Humans," is that "there is no discernible line to be drawn between making inheritable repair of genetic defects and improving the species." The *Times* rightly points out that once scientists are able to repair genetic defects, "it will become much harder to argue against additional genes that confer desired qualities, like better health, looks, or brains."

If diabetes, sickle cell anemia, and cancer are to be prevented by altering the genetic makeup of individuals, why not proceed to other less serious "defects": myopia, color blindness, dyslexia, obesity, left-handedness? Indeed, what is to preclude the world from deciding that a certain skin color is a disorder? In the end, why would we ever say no to any alteration of the genetic code that might enhance the well-being of our offspring? It would be difficult to imagine parents rejecting genetic modifications that promised to improve, in some way, the opportunities for their progeny.

Despite the growing enthusiasm among some molecular biologists for engineering fundamental changes in the genetic code of human sex cells, it should be emphasized that treating genetic disorders by eliminating them at the germ line level is far different from treating genetic disorders by way of somatic gene surgery after birth. In the former instance, the genetic deletions can result, in the long run, in a dangerous narrowing of the human gene pool, which future generations rely on for making evolutionary adaptations to changing environments. On the other hand, if somatic gene surgery proves to be a safe, therapeutic way to treat serious diseases that cannot be effectively treated by more conventional approaches, it would appear to have potential value.

Perfecting the Code

While the notion of consumer choice would appear benign, the very idea of eliminating so-called genetic defects raises the troubling question of what is meant by the term "defective." Ethicist Daniel Callahan of the Hastings Center penetrates to the core of the problem when he observes that "behind the human horror at genetic defectiveness lurks ... an image of the perfect human being. The very language of 'defect,' 'abnormality,' 'disease,' and 'risk' presupposes such an image, a kind of proto-type of perfection."

The very idea of engineering the human species—by making changes at the germ line level—is not too dissimilar from the idea of engineering a piece of machinery. An engineer is constantly in search of new ways to improve the performance of a machine. As soon as one set of defects is eliminated, the engineer immediately turns his attention to the next set of defects, always with the idea in mind of creating a more efficient machine. The very idea of setting arbitrary limits as to how much "improvement" is acceptable is alien to the entire conception of engineering.

The new language of the information sciences has transformed many molecular biologists from scientists to engineers, although they are, no doubt, scarcely aware of the metamorphosis. When molecular biologists speak of mutations and genetic diseases as errors in the code, the implicit, if not explicit, assumption is that they should never have existed in the first place, that they are "bugs," or mistakes that need to be deprogrammed or corrected. The molecular biologist, in turn, becomes the computing engineer, the writer of codes, continually eliminating errors and reprogramming instructions to upgrade both the program and the performance. This is a dubious and dangerous role when we stop to consider that every human being brings with him or her a number of lethal recessive genes. Do we then come to see ourselves as miswired from the get-go, riddled with errors in our code? If that is the case, against what ideal norm of perfection are we to be measured? If every human being is made up of varying degrees of error, then we search in vain for the norm, the ideal. What makes the new language of molecular biology so subtly chilling is that it risks creating a new archetype, a flawless, errorless, perfect being to which to aspire—a new man and woman, like us, but without the warts, wrinkles, vulnerabilities, and frailties that have defined humanity's essence from the very beginning of our existence.

No wonder so many in the disability rights community are becoming increasingly frightened of the new biology. They wonder, if in this new world, people like themselves will be seen as errors in the code, mistakes to be eliminated, lives to be prevented from coming into being. We are not likely to be tolerant when we come to see everyone around us as defective.

The question, then, is whether or not humanity should begin the process of engineering future generations of human beings by technological design in the laboratory. What are the potential consequences of embarking on a course whose final goal is the "perfection" of the human species?

Is Opposition to Gene Therapy Futile?

Many in the life sciences field would have us believe that the new gene splicing technologies are irrepressible and irreversible and that any attempt to oppose their introduction is both futile and retrogressive. They never stop to even consider the possibility that the new genetic science might be used in a wholly different manner than is currently being proposed.

While the global life science companies favor the introduction and widespread use of gene therapy to cure diseases and enhance the physical, emotional, and mental well-being of individuals, a growing number of holistically-minded geneticists and health practitioners are beginning to use the new data generated by the Human Genome Project in a very different way. They are exploring the relationship between genetic mutations and environmental triggers with the hope of fashioning a more sophisticated, scientifically-based understanding and approach to international health. More than 70 percent of all deaths in the United States and other industrialized countries are attributable to what physicians refer to as "diseases of affluence." Heart attacks, strokes, diabetes, and breast, colon, and prostate cancer are among the most common diseases of affluence. While each individual has varying genetic susceptibilities to these diseases, environmental factors, including diet and lifestyle, are major contributing elements that can trigger genetic mutations. Heavy cigarette smoking, high levels of alcohol consumption, diets rich in animal fats, the use of pesticides and other poisonous chemicals, contaminated water and food, polluted air, and sedentary living habits with little or no exercise, have been shown in study after study to cause genetic mutations and lead to the onset of many of these high profile diseases.

The mapping and sequencing of the human genome is providing researchers with vital new information on recessive gene traits and genetic predispositions for a range of illnesses. Still, little research has been done, to date, on how genetic predispositions interact with toxic materials in the environment, the metabolism of different foods, and lifestyle to affect genetic mutations and phenotypic expression. The new holistic approach to human medicine views the individual genome as part of an embedded organismic structure, continually interacting with and being affected by the environment in which it unfolds. The effort is geared toward using increasingly sophisticated genetic and environmental information to prevent genetic mutations from occurring.

The new "soft path" approach to the age of biology represents a change in the way researchers harness the new scientific and technological breakthroughs in the genetic sciences. While the "hard path" approach favors using the new genetic science to engineer changes in the very blueprint of a human being to advance medical progress, the soft path uses the same genetic information to create a more sustainable relationship between individual human beings and their environments. Although there is certainly a growing market for preventive health practices, programs, and products, far more money is invested in "illness-based" medicine. That could change, but it would require a paradigm shift in the way we think about science and its applications.

In closing, the biotech revolution will affect many aspects of our lives. The way we eat, the way we date and marry, the way we have our babies, the way our children are raised and educated, the way we perceive the world around us and our place in it—many of our individual and shared realities will be deeply touched by the new technologies of the Biotech Century. Surely, these very "personal" technologies deserve to be widely discussed and debated by the public at large before they become a ubiquitous part of our daily lives.

Silencing Bad Genes

Anthony Komaroff and Judy Lieberman

Anthony Komaroff and Judy Lieberman are professors at Harvard Medical School. In the following selection they describe the new technique in genetic engineering known as gene silencing. Many biologists consider this one of the most exciting developments of the twenty-first century. Scientists are learning how to silence specific genes—that is, to prevent these genes, either temporarily or permanently, from having any effect on the organism. This is done by making use of a recently discovered mechanism involving RNA (ribonucleic acid) known as RNA interference (sometimes called RNAi). It has been found that RNA, which is made by DNA, does more than had previously been thought; it is involved in gene expression and regulation. RNA interference enables scientists to learn about the functions of genes by silencing them to see what happens when they are not expressed. In addition it may lead to an entirely new class of drugs to treat human diseases.

A 6-year-old boy is suddenly engulfed by pain. It is his first attack; he will suffer repeated agony, along with breathlessness and debilitating fatigue, for the rest of his short life. Over the course of a few days, a 35-year-old lawyer loses her appetite and energy, then the whites of her eyes turn yellow. Trying to open a stuck window, a 55-year-old nurse feels a sudden sharp pain just above her wrist. The bone has broken, weakened by cancer cells that have silently spread there from her breast, and are multiplying uncontrollably.

In each case, wayward genes are the culprit. The boy inherited a defective gene that makes a misshapen version of the hemoglobin protein inside his red blood cells, causing sickle-cell anemia. The lawyer has been infected by a hepatitis virus that has commandeered her liver cells, instructing them to make proteins from viral genes instead of from human genes. The nurse inherited a breast-cancer gene from her Ashkenazi Jewish parents, and the gene is ordering the cells to multiply.

Doctors have long dreamed of a magic bullet that could travel harmlessly through the body to diseased cells, enter those cells and switch off the wayward genes that cause the suffering. Now, new research holds out hope for just such a treatment, through a technique called RNA interference. Since the 1960s it has been the central tenet of biology that a specific sequence of DNA (a gene) makes a specific sequence of messenger RNA, which in turn makes a specific protein. This profoundly important insight led to an important question, however. What controls that process? All our genes are contained in each of our cells. But in each cell, certain genes are expressed while others remain dormant, which is why the trillions of cells in the human body look and function differently from one another.

Over the past 30 years, scientists have identified various proteins that activate or silence genes. However, those proteins are large and complex molecules that are difficult to harness in order to control disease. The surprise breakthrough came in 1990. A team of plant scientists at the University of California, Davis, and a company called DNA Plant Technology were trying to make a purple petunia even more purple by inserting into it a gene for purple pigment. Instead of turning a deeper purple, however, some of the flowers were pale white and others were mottled. The researchers discovered that the inserted gene had stimulated the production of very small RNAs, and that these microRNAs shut down the gene activity that led to the production of purple pigment. Other scientists then found microRNAs in primitive animals and in humans. The microRNA attaches to the messenger RNA and destroys it before it can produce its designated protein, thus "interfering with" or "silencing" the instructions of the gene.

From Curiosity to Cure

Considered just a curiosity at first, RNA interference has since revolutionized biological research. It allows scientists to silence specific genes very precisely in cell cultures and even in animals, like mice. Since science has now identified every gene in humans, in several animals and in many microorganisms that cause human disease, researchers can systematically silence one gene after another, and observe what happens to the cells or the animals—a direct test of a gene's function, including its role in causing a particular disease. If a gene plays such a role, it becomes a target for developing a conventional or novel drug treatment.

Could microRNA technology lead to the magic bullet—drugs that silence wayward genes? It's easy enough to produce microRNAs that silence a particular gene. Such synthetically made RNAs are called small interfering RNAs, or siRNAs. The hard part is delivering the siRNA to the cells deep inside the body, where the wayward genes are causing mayhem. But progress is being made. Scientists are figuring out ways to protect the siRNAs from destruction as they circulate through the body, and to allow them entry into the target cells. In animal studies, siRNAs have stifled autoimmune hepatitis, a neurological disease called spinocerebellar ataxia, several viral diseases and several types of cancer, and have dramatically lowered cholesterol levels. And, in human studies, siRNAs have recently shown promise in the treatment of macular degeneration, the leading cause of blindness in the elderly.

It's true that we already have conventional drugs that inhibit the reproduction of some viruses, slow the growth of cancer and lower cholesterol. But RNA-interference technology offers a number of advantages. For one thing, there are many pathological genes for which no counteracting drugs have yet been developed. And while the process of looking for conventional drugs that counteract the effects of wayward genes is getting faster and more efficient, it's still ponderous and expensive. Once scientists know the identity and structure of a wayward gene, they can easily make siRNAs to silence it. And, compared with most conventional drugs, siRNAs are simple molecules that should be very inexpensive to produce. Also, since the immune system does not recognize siRNAs as foreign, they would likely produce fewer side effects than conventional drugs.

Obstacles to Overcome

Though there are reasons to be optimistic that this new technology will lead to powerful and nontoxic new treatments, there are many obstacles to overcome. It remains to be seen whether siRNAs will be able to reach all their potential targets deep in the body. And there is the possibility of collateral damage; some siRNAs may silence not only a wayward gene but several healthy genes with similar structures as well. It is also uncertain how durable the effect of this new form of therapy will be. It's possible that in chronic diseases, siRNAs, like conventional treatments, will need to be given repeatedly in order to sustain a beneficial effect. Eventually, gene therapy may be used to express microRNAs throughout a patient's life, but gene therapy has been plagued by difficulties.

While the value of RNA-interference therapy in humans remains to be proved, the story of its discovery is just the latest example of how an investment in basic research can lead to completely unexpected, and enormously beneficial, results. Who could have imagined that trying to make a petunia more purple would reveal a potential new approach for shutting down the growth of cancer? No one. That's why it's wise for a society to invest in curious people who try to understand how living things work.

A Mother Tells Why She Would Not Want Her Child Changed by Gene Therapy

Clare Ferguson

Clare Ferguson is a publicist with Wilfred Laurier University Press and the book review editor of Voices Across Boundaries, *a Canadian publication. In the following selection she tells about her son, who has Down syndrome, and explains why she does not agree with people who believe that this disease should be eliminated by genetic testing or gene therapy. She feels that her son's disabilities are part of him and could not be removed without changing his personality. In Ferguson's opinion, the common focus on eliminating imperfection is misguided and the money now spent on prenatal diagnosis through genetic testing would be better spent in other ways.*

Down syndrome [DS] is a genetic condition that causes delays in physical and intellectual development. It is the most common chromosomal disorder, occurring in approximately one in every 800 live births.

People born with Down syndrome have 47 chromosomes instead of the usual 46. As children, they are usually smaller than other children, and their physical and mental development is slower. They vary widely in mental abilities and developmental progress, with most of them functioning in the mild to moderate range of developmental disability. Their motor development is slow; and instead of walking by 12 to 14 months as other children do, they usually learn to walk between 15 and 36 months. Language development is also markedly delayed.

Sixty to 80 percent of children with Down syndrome have hearing deficits, and 40 to 45 percent have congenital heart disease. Many of these children will have to undergo cardiac surgery and often they will need long-term care by a pediatric cardiologist. Thyroid dysfunctions are more common in children with Down syndrome (between 15 and 20 percent have hypothyroidism), as are upper respiratory illnesses.

Down syndrome is not related to race, nationality, religion or socioeconomic status. Despite the statistics, with appropriate health care, children born with this disorder can expect to live productive and healthy lives. Most children with Down syndrome live with their families and many are included in regular classroom settings. As adults and young adults, many hold jobs in the community and some pursue higher education at community colleges. All are individuals who make valuable contributions to society.

I was going to begin by stating that the day Russell was born was a day that changed my life forever. Technically, though, that's not true. For almost a full year I remained blissfully unaware that Russell was not "perfect." When he was born, the doctor who delivered him had a suspicion of Down syndrome and asked the pediatrician on call to have a look. Only after the pediatrician had decided that the initial suspicion was groundless did they tell me they had "checked him over, but not to worry—he's fine." I was happy to accept their diagnosis and I put the issue out of my mind. Not once in the following months did I think that they could have been wrong, and it never came up at monthly medical appointments.

In the course of a regular one-year checkup, my family doctor confessed that she had been "keeping an eye on Russell" and would like to send him for blood tests to confirm Down syndrome. This happened without Russell's father present, and in front of my two older children. To say I was dumbfounded is an understatement. Russell had been delayed in his development, but not noticeably so. The tests were done; Russell was diagnosed with Down syndrome.

Russell's father and I were whisked off to McMaster Medical Centre for genetic testing. This testing seemed to be supremely important to all the doctors involved. How did this happen? What are the chances of its happening again? They took blood from both of us and presented us with all the karyotype possibilities. The mood was sombre and I remember feeling vaguely confused and angry, though I couldn't find a voice to express that. Because of the specific makeup of Russell's chromosomes it was possible that he could have inherited his Down syndrome from one of us. As it turned out, neither of us was "responsible" for Russell's Down syndrome. We now had the same chance of having another baby with DS as any other family that has one child with DS: 1 in 100.

We returned to see the pediatrician who had misdiagnosed Russell at birth. He was extremely nervous, and spent a lot of time listening to the murmur in Russell's heart. About 40 percent of children with DS are born with a congenital heart defect, usually surgically repaired, often in the first year of life—an opportunity that had passed us by. About twenty minutes into the appointment, after watching the doctor shake and stutter, I said, "You know, Dr. Jones [not his real name], I am not going to sue you." He looked embarrassed, but he visibly relaxed. I couldn't believe it. Here we were trying to find out the medical needs of our baby, and he's shaking in his boots in fear of a lawsuit. I changed pediatricians shortly afterward. Russell's heart turned out to be fine and, on the whole, he is a very healthy little boy.

The full impact of being Russell's mother may not have started at birth but it didn't take long after his diagnosis for me to change my outlook on life. My experience with the medical profession had left me angry and has led me to advocacy. Through Russell's needs, I found a voice to speak up. This continued when Russell started school, and it served me well when I was pregnant with my youngest child.

Having another child was something that I had been wrestling with. I strongly believed that a younger sibling would be good for Russell. Being the youngest of three children as well as being "special" might put too much focus on him. When I described my struggle, most people thought I was crazy. Having a fourth child was seen as self-indulgent, and the question always came up, "What if you have another one?" This came from people I love, who love me. My doctor was fairly blunt in her advice to quit while I was ahead. Still, the pull was strong and I did become pregnant again. Immediately, medical testing became an issue. Never before had I had any sort of screening test, but suddenly it was required. I said no. I then had to sign a form saying I had refused testing. My entire pregnancy felt surreal. Complete strangers, seeing me with Russell, would question my decision to have another child. I got tired of defending what I thought was a personal decision. Eventually I stopped and resorted to blank stares of incomprehension which made them uncomfortable enough to go away.

A few years ago, *Chatelaine* magazine ran a feature called "Making the Perfect Baby." It was a fairly balanced article but the comments of some of the people interviewed incensed me enough to write a letter to the editor. They seemed to indicate that everyone wants a "perfect" baby and that it is selfish to bring a child into the world who can't enjoy "quality of life." One argument for testing was the early detection of abnormality for easier termination or treatment. Current statistics show the rate of termination in pregnancies where the fetus has been diagnosed with DS is more than 90 percent. Clearly, this is the main reason for earlier and earlier testing. As a parent it makes me sad, not because I don't believe in reproductive choice but because Russell has brought me so much joy. Almost every family I know that has a child with DS talks of the huge amounts of love and joy that surround their child. It saddens me that Down syndrome is still seen as such a deficit that more than 90 percent of people choose not to bring a baby diagnosed with DS into the world.

The completion of the Human Genome Project has engendered exciting possibilities in research and treatment. "Gene therapy" is touted as a cure-all. Down syndrome has been mentioned. If I could reduce, without risky and intrusive treatment, the challenges my son faces as a result of his having DS, I wouldn't think twice. It has been my life's mission to facilitate the best life possible for Russell and I work on it every day through advocacy and education. However, erasing Down syndrome from Russell—removing all characteristics belonging to Down syndrome but not to Russell—is impossible. He is a whole person, not a sum of his parts. How do you separate his goofy personality and his huge capacity for love from his terrifying complete lack of fear of strangers? His trust in people is partly a result of his limited intellectual abilities. If you remove the intellectual challenge, does the same person remain? I don't know. Is it even fair of me to impose on Russell my wish for him to stay as he is? How do his rights figure into it? These are very hard questions and, in a way, I'm glad that I won't have to answer them in my lifetime.

It has been a few years since I wrote my highly indignant letter to *Chatelaine* magazine, and time has tempered my response. However, I find my position on genetic testing unchanged. The focus on eliminating imperfection seems misguided to me. In my opinion, as a parent of a child with a developmental disability, the increasing amounts of money spent on early diagnosis would be better spent on the education and health needs of all children and the education of society towards acceptance of difference. As for Russell, I think I was right ten years ago when I thought he was perfect. He is.

A Patient Tells Why He Believes Gene Therapy Is Worth Calculated Risks

Eric Kast

The following selection is a portion of the testimony given to a committee of the U.S. Senate by Eric Kast, a cystic fibrosis patient who at the age of six was a "poster child" for the state of Indiana. As an adult he volunteered to participate in a clinical trial of gene therapy for cystic fibrosis in the hope of contributing to the search for a cure. In his testimony he explained the problems of living with this disease and why, in his opinion and that of the Cystic Fibrosis Foundation, it is important that the calculated risks of gene therapy research be taken.

Thank you for inviting me to speak to you today. My name is Eric Kast. I was diagnosed with cystic fibrosis (CF) when I was three months old, so I have never known what it is like not to have CF. I also participated in a clinical trial for gene therapy.

Today, I would like to share with you my thoughts and experiences about gene therapy, and the views of the Cystic Fibrosis Foundation on regulatory oversight for gene therapy. In summary: Gene therapy must continue to move forward as quickly as possible as it offers me and the 30,000 others with CF a realistic hope for the ultimate cure. . . .

Living with CF

Cystic fibrosis is a genetic disease that primarily affects the lungs. My body produces thick, sticky mucus that clogs the airways and is difficult to cough up. Because of this, I am more susceptible to frequent lung infections, which will even-

Eric Kast, testimony before the U.S. Senate Subcommittee on Public Health, Committee on Health, Education, Labor and Pensions, Washington, DC, February 2, 2000.

tually destroy my airways. To fight these lung infections, I take antibiotics intravenously. CF also affects my digestive system, so I take pills with each meal to digest my food. When I was 31, I also developed diabetes as a result of CF, so I now take insulin shots.

Compared to a healthy person who enjoys close to 100 percent of lung capacity, my lung function scores are about 40 percent. Every day presents a struggle to breathe for me and the 30,000 other people in the United States who also have cystic fibrosis. Despite this constant battle, I am fortunate. I'm still alive. I'm 33 while the current life expectancy for someone with CF is only 32. In short, I have outlived my life expectancy and I am in a race against this disease. A life expectancy of 32 years is simply unacceptable.

It is not easy for me to stay healthy. Between exercise, physical therapy to clear my lungs and breathing treatments, like Pulmozyme® to thin the mucus and albuterol to open the airways, it takes me two hours each day just to maintain my health. Approved in 1993, Pulmozyme® was the first drug ever to be approved specifically for CF. However, I live with the knowledge that, any day, my health could be taken away. Two years ago, a friend of mine with CF who was 24 was healthier than I was. Six months later, he was on a waiting list for a lung transplant, and eight months after that, he was dead. This tragic story can be told time and again by those who have known someone with CF.

People such as my friend who lost his battle and my 5-year-old niece, Kelsey, who also has CF, are my motivation to participate in clinical research. Since I was 22, I have volunteered for eight clinical trials, including a gene therapy trial about 3½ years ago. I have participated in clinical trials near my home in Norman, Oklahoma, as well as in Maryland at the National Institutes of Health (NIH), and at Johns Hopkins University.

I have also been active in the CF community since I was six years old when I was "poster child" for the state of Indiana. One of the highlights of my life was July 3, 1974 when it was proclaimed "Eric Kast Day" in Indianapolis by then-Mayor Richard Lugar—now one of your colleagues. Another highlight of my life—and one of the things I'm proudest of—is my participation in these pioneering gene therapy studies. Growing up, I was active in every CF fund-raising event from bowl-a-ramas to swim-a-thons. However, as I got older, I was not as comfortable asking people for money. I began volunteering for research studies and gene therapy as my way to contribute to the search for a cure for cystic fibrosis.

Indeed, we are in a race to find a cure and we will achieve this only through strong medical research. We are at a crossroads in history right now. We can continue with gene therapy—with appropriate caution—or we can let fear of the unknown paralyze us into inaction. Inaction would result in the tragic loss of those of us with CF. My greatest personal fear is that a cure will come out just a year or two too late for me. My wife, Sherry, will have to live the rest of her life knowing that if I could have just made it one more year, I would have won the race and we would live happily for the next 30, 40, or 50 years. We have come that far and we really are that close for me to believe I could celebrate a 40th or 50th wedding anniversary. It is clinical trials into promising research, such as gene therapy, that will help me make this dream a reality. . . .

My Experience with Clinical Trials

Fighting every day for a healthy tomorrow, the cure cannot come fast enough—for me or for the Foundation. We all recognize that research will never be without risk. Informing patients of these risks is paramount. Only then can volunteers like me make educated decisions about whether or not to participate in research.

I would like to read to you a portion of the informed consent document I signed before agreeing to participate in the gene therapy trial using the adeno-associated virus vector [AAV] at Johns Hopkins University:

> "We do not know what the risks are when people are given the altered AAV virus with the CFTR gene. The altered virus could spread to other parts of your body—the consequences of this are not known at this time. There is a very small chance that the altered virus could damage the DNA in the cells of your lungs or nose. If this happened, it could put you at risk for developing cancer in the future. You will receive no therapeutic benefit from this. Side effects in humans are not known. If you should die either during or after this study, we will ask your family for permission for an autopsy."

I think that is a pretty clear and strong statement. I relied on my knowledge of the research and a great amount of trust in the scientists and physicians who were confident in what they were about to do. I also had to trust recent history. When I entered the trial, ten people who had already participated in this trial had not experienced any side effects. Fortunately, I experienced no side effects either.

Some may argue that people like me cannot agree to participate in a trial, like gene therapy. They may think that signing up for a trial which brings serious risk of illness or death is more an emotional choice devoid of reason, because of our "desperation" to find a cure. On the contrary, I know what I am risking—my future with my family—and I know that I must take these risks to give my niece and the 30,000 others with CF the chance I never really had to live a long, healthy life. We are all in this together—and we win or lose together. Research is the only hope we have for beating this disease forever.

The most important issue for volunteers in a study is safety. I want to know what other volunteers have experienced in the trials and if there were any adverse reactions linked to each study. I know that numerous tests were done before I was accepted in each trial to ensure I was healthy enough to participate. If I thought that researchers were not telling me everything, I would not participate. Informed consent is just that—informed.

Another critical issue is confidentiality of medical information. However, different people have different comfort levels. I want people to know about CF, so I often share my story. However, I do not want every stranger knowing details of my health condition. Specific medical information about volunteers should only be available to researchers who are working directly with the patient. If the information were to become public, other family members or employers who might not know about the patient's health condition might use it to discriminate.

My decision to participate in a study is simply—my decision. In all of the studies I have been fortunate enough to participate in, I know the researchers had my best interests at heart and that my health was their number one concern. I have been given the option to leave a study at any time. . . .

Gene therapy must continue to move forward as quickly as possible as it offers me and the 30,000 others with CF a realistic hope for the ultimate cure. I am confident in the FDA [Food and Drug Administration], the CF Foundation, and the researchers that they are taking all steps necessary to ensure that clinical trials are as safe as possible and will act quickly to address new risks or halt a trial if necessary.

Calculated Risks Must Be Taken

The local CF community and my family and friends in Oklahoma look to me as a role model and as a source of information and hope because of my participation in these trials. They see this as my strong commitment to a cure. When the media reports on research, I often get calls from anxious parents who are looking for hope for their child's future. Everyone, particularly those of us living with a life-threatening illness, deserves hope for the future. Gene therapy provides one of the greatest hopes for my future.

As I described earlier, I battle every day in my fight against CF. The CF Foundation, scientists, doctors, even the FDA, and now you, honorable senators, are my partners in this battle. All of us take calculated risks every day. We get into our car and drive to work hoping the driver next to us does not cause an accident and injure us. With gene therapy, patients like me must take calculated risks. We do all we can to minimize the risks—just as you would wear your seat belt to help prevent injury.

But as someone who has participated in eight clinical trials, including gene therapy, I am willing to make informed decisions, and take those risks to contribute to better treatments and an eventual cure for cystic fibrosis. My battle with CF is a race. Don't let me lose that race when the finish line might be just around the corner. Thank you.

CHAPTER 3

Genetic Enhancement of Human Abilities

Genetic Enhancement of Humans Raises Troubling Questions

Sally Deneen

*Sally Deneen is a freelance writer who lives in Seattle. In the fol-
lowing selection she describes some of the predictions that have
been made about genetic enhancement of humans and some of
the problems that such enhancement might cause. Opponents,
she states, say that it would be risky and would require long experimentation involving many malformed babies and miscarriages. Others call for a ban on the modification of genes passed
to children, even if it becomes safe, because they feel it would
change people into products or would violate basic environmental and ethical principles. Another objection often raised is that
those who could not afford gene enrichment might be relegated
to second-class citizenship. However, Deneen reports, some opponents recognize that advocates of human enhancement include
powerful and influential people who will not give up easily.*

Princeton University microbiologist Lee M. Silver can see a
day a few centuries from now when there are two species
of humans—the standard-issue "Naturals," and the "Gene-
enriched," an elite class whose parents consciously bought for
them designer genes, and whose parents before them did the
same, and so on for generations. Want Billy to have superior
athletic ability? Plunk down the cash. Want Suzy to be excep-
tionally smart? Just pull out the Visa card at your local fertil-
ity clinic, where the elite likely will go to enhance their babies-
to-be.

It will start innocently enough: Birth defects that are
caused by a single gene, such as cystic fibrosis and Tay-Sachs

disease, will be targeted first, and probably with little controversy. Then, as societal fears about messing with Mother Nature subside, Silver and other researchers predict that a genetic
solution to preventing diabetes, heart disease and other big
killers will be found and offered. So will genetic inoculations
against HIV. Eventually, the mind will be targeted for improvement—preventing alcohol addiction and mental illness,
and enhancing visual acuity or intelligence to try to produce
the next Vincent Van Gogh or Albert Einstein. Even traits
from other animals may be added, such as a dog's sense of
smell or an eagle's eyesight.

What parents would see as a simple, if pricey, way to improve their kids would result, after many generations of gene
selection, in a profound change by the year 2400—humans
would be two distinct species, related as humans and chimps
are today, and just as unable to interbreed. People now have
46 chromosomes; the gene-enriched would have 48 to accom-
modate added traits, Silver predicts in his aptly titled book,
Remaking Eden. . . .

An Accelerating Timetable

How soon will all this happen? Silver believes that by around
2010 parents will be able to genetically ensure their babies
won't grow up to be fat or alcoholic, and by 2050 arrange to
insert an extra gene into single-cell embryos within 24 hours
of conception to make babies resistant to AIDS. It is already
possible to insert foreign DNA into mice, pigs and sheep. The
obstacles to inserting them in humans are mainly technical
ones. At this point in human knowledge, it could lead to mutations. Several techniques are under development to try to
avoid that, however.

"For the near and midterm future, we're looking at science
fiction. You'd have to be terminally reckless to do that type of
human engineering on people [with what we know now]," argues law professor Henry T. Greely, co-director of the Pro-

gram in Genomics, Ethics and Society at the Stanford University Center for Biomedical Ethics.

To change a baby's eye color or hair color within a fertilized human egg "would be a very expensive and dangerous proposition for such trivial purposes," says Dr. Marvin Frazier, who fields human genome questions as director of the Life Sciences Division of the U.S. Department of Energy's Office of Biological and Environmental Research. "It is also my opinion that this would be wrong," he added, "but that will not stop some people from wanting to try."

As for manipulating intelligence or athletic ability, Frazier says it will take scientists many decades to figure out how to do it. These particular traits don't rely on one gene, but on all genes. They also rely "to a significant degree" on nurture instead of nature. Even when scientists figure it out, "It is likely that to achieve the desired goals would require a lot of experimentation, which translates into many hundred or thousands of mistakes before you get it right." That means, Frazier says, "a lot of malformed babies and miscarriages."

A Pivotal Moment

To University of Washington professor Phil Bereano, among others, now is the time for all of us to talk with friends and colleagues to hash out the ethical and societal implications of this Brave New World. Do we really want to commodify people? Could it be a Pandora's box? Unfortunately, the box may already be open: Many nations have banned genetic engineering on humans, but the United States has not.

"If scientists don't play God, who will?" said supporter James Watson, former head of the Human Genome Project, speaking before the British Parliamentary and Scientific Committee in June [2000]. "The key question is not whether human [genetic] manipulation will occur, but how and when it will," says a confident Gregory Stock, director of UCLA's Program on Science, Technology and Society in a report entitled, "The Prospects for Human Germline Engineering."

Meanwhile, a long-anticipated September [2000] report by the American Association for the Advancement of Science (AAAS) surprised some observers by failing to call for a ban on making inheritable genetic changes in humans—that is, genetic changes that would be carried on by progeny. Indeed, while the report says that such research "cannot presently be carried out safely and responsibly on human beings," it also leaves wiggle room. "Human trials of inheritable genetic changes should not be initiated until reliable techniques for gene correction or replacement are developed that meet agreed-upon standards for safety and efficacy," says report co-author Mark Frankel, director of AAAS' Scientific Freedom, Responsibility and Law Program.

Noting the public outcry after the cloning of Dolly the sheep—which raised the possibility of cloned human beings—the report stresses the importance of public discussion about genetic research before major technical innovations occur. So instead of a ban, the report suggests "rigorous analysis and public dialogue."

But there's no shortage of opposition to human engineering. The San Francisco–based Exploratory Initiative on the New Human Genetic Technologies seeks, among other things, to alert a largely unwitting public to what is going on. "It really is a nightmare vision," says Rich Hayes, who coordinates the campaign from his Public Media Center office. "Once we start genetically re-engineering human beings, where would we stop? We should have the maturity and wisdom to ban the modification of the genes we pass to our children."

Designer Genes

The futuristic notion of choosing a child's genes from a catalog can certainly capture the imagination. Just as parents today enroll their children in the best possible schools and pay for orthodontics, the parents of the future—perhaps in a few decades—would be able to choose from an ever-increasing suite of traits: hair color, eye color, bigger muscles and so on.

Maybe they'd like to add a few inches to a child's height. Or improve a kid's chances at longevity by tweaking inherited DNA. Or ensure a resistance to viruses. Neighborhood clinics could, by appointment, insert a block of genes into a newly fertilized egg. As one cell broke into two, then four, and so on, each cell would contain the new traits. And the child would pass on those traits to all subsequent generations. Who could blame parents for going for this?

But to Stuart Newman, professor of cell biology and anatomy at New York Medical College in Valhalla, New York, the effect on human biology could be analogous to transforming wild areas into artificial areas, or wild food into artificial food.

We "might be changing people into products—genetically engineered products," says Newman, who also is chairman of the Human Genetics Committee for the Council for Responsible Genetics in Cambridge, Massachusetts. "That's something that's opened up by the Humane Genome Project."

"We believe that certain activities in the area of genetics and cloning should be prohibited because they violate basic environmental and ethical principles," Friends of the Earth President Brent Blackwelder and Physicians for Social Responsibility Executive Director Robert Musil said in a 1999 joint statement. "The idea of redesigning human beings and animals to suit the primarily commercial goals of a limited number of individuals is fundamentally at odds with the principle of respect for nature."

Proponents and critics alike envision a future in which those who can't afford gene enrichment will be relegated to second-class citizenship. "As far as I'm concerned, this thrill we have about the future will end up being one big elitist ripple," says Beth Burrows, director of the Edmonds Institute, a suburban Seattle nonprofit institute that works on issues related to environment, technology, ethics and law.

The Green Dimension

And what about the environment? Burrows says several important questions arise about genetic tampering: What are we creating? How will it affect the natural world? What will be the effect on evolution for each species involved? How will it change feeding patterns, or food for other animals? Without understanding interactions, she says, "We may do some extremely stupid things. If people are concerned that there was such a severe backlash against genetically modified foods, I think they haven't seen anything compared to the backlash when we are able to alter the human genome in significant ways—even insignificant ways," says Burrows.

UCLA's Gregory Stock agrees the impact of human genetic modification is profound, but he likes it. "This technology will force us to re-examine even the very notion of what it means to be human," he wrote in a recent report. "For as we become subject to the same process of conscious design that has so dramatically altered the world around us, we will be unable to avoid looking at what distinguishes us from other life, at how our genetics shapes us, at how much we are willing to intervene in life's flow from parent to child."

Ignacio Chapela of the University of California at Berkeley is troubled by still other implications the Human Genome Project may bring for the natural world—including plants engineered specifically to produce human proteins, and pigs produced to have antigens that are more human-like in a quest to help humans. To Chapela, a professor in the Department of Environmental Science, Policy and Management, the concept, say, of using chimpanzees as surrogate mothers for human embryos is "abhorrent—degrading for chimpanzees, and for humans, as well. I think what we're talking about is a very deep understanding of what it means to be part of an intricate web of life, and why we have boundaries between species." To Chapela, proponents see the world as a sphere smeared with mix-and-match DNA. "Evolutionarily, it makes sense to have boundaries," he says, "and we're just willy-nilly breaking them down.". . .

A Brave New World

UCLA's Stock isn't concerned about the effects of human genetic engineering on nature. "Even if half the world's species were lost, enormous diversity would still remain," he argues in his 1993 book, *Metaman: The Merging of Humans and Machines into a Global Superorganism.* "We best serve ourselves, as well as future generations, by focusing on the short-term consequences of our actions rather than our vague notions about the needs of the distant future—if medical science develops an easy cure for cancer, [nuclear] wastes may not be viewed as a significant health hazard after all. If robots can be employed to safely concentrate and reprocess the radioactive materials, they might even be valuable."

Not so fast, says another architect of the modern world, Bill Joy, the father of Java software and co-founder of Sun Microsystems. Joy posits with some feeling of guilt that "our most powerful 21st-century technologies are threatening to make humans an endangered species." In a celebrated article in *Wired* magazine, Joy blamed the possible extinction of humans on a few key causes, including genetic engineering and robotics. Artificial intelligence should match that of humans within 20 or 30 years.

To combat the perceived inevitability of this Brave New World, Marcy Darnovsky, a Sonoma State University instructor who works with the Exploratory Initiative on the New Human Genetic Technologies, calls for three things: First, a global ban on inheritable genetic engineering on humans; second, a global ban on human reproductive cloning; and third, an effective and accountable regulation of other human genetic technologies.

Burrows says we need to be pondering such weighty questions as: Do we really want to merge with machines? "There are tremendous—awful—choices to be made," she says. "It's very risky to have these discussions because they're about common values. The subject is difficult, painful and easily avoided. But we have to stop focusing on the science and think of ourselves as part of an ecosystem."

Chapela is also worried about the lack of civic discourse. But the advocates are talking, particularly among themselves. At a Berkeley conference, one of them, Extropy Institute President Max More, stood before the crowd and read an open letter to Mother Nature:

> Sorry to disturb you, but we humans—your offspring—come to you with some things to say:
>
> You have raised us from simple self-replicating chemicals to trillion-celled mammals;
>
> What you have made us is glorious, yet deeply flawed;
>
> We will no longer tolerate the tyranny of aging and death. Through genetic alterations, cellular manipulations, synthetic organs, and any necessary means, we will endow ourselves with enduring vitality and remove our expiration date.

Other proponents are more sober, and include Nobel laureate scientists. "This is no 'marginal' movement or way of thinking," Chapela says. "The group advocating human re-engineering includes extremely powerful, influential and wealthy people. So don't expect them to roll over easily or soon."

Genetic Enhancement Will Not Limit Human Freedom

Ronald Bailey

Ronald Bailey is a science correspondent for Reason *magazine. His articles have appeared in many magazines and he is the author of several books, most recently* Liberation Biology: The Scientific and Moral Case for the Biotech Revolution. *In the following selection he argues that although opponents of genetic enhancement have said that it would restrict human freedom and turn people into semiprogrammed robots, that claim is based on genetic essentialism: the idea that human individuality depends entirely on genes. As Bailey explains, this idea is false. Furthermore, he says, to the extent that human characteristics do depend on genes, they are already predetermined; parents merely do not know as much about what genes they are conferring on their children as they would if they could choose them. To the objection that genetically enhanced children would have no choice about what genes they were born with, he replies that children have never had any choice. As for the common worry that genetic enhancement would result in political inequality or lack of tolerance, equality before the law does not now depend on biology, and, in Bailey's opinion, there is no reason why the principles that apply today would change.*

One might be tempted to dismiss concerns about genetic enhancement as premature. However, even bioconservatives like Francis Fukuyama don't think so. "As we discover not just correlations but actual molecular pathways between genes and traits like intelligence, aggression, sexual identity, criminality, alcoholism, and the like, it will inevitably occur to people that they can make use of this knowledge for particular social ends," worries Fukuyama in his book *Our Posthu-*

man Future. "This will play itself out as a series of ethical questions facing individual parents, and also as a political issue that may someday come to dominate politics."

The prospect of a safe biotechnology that enables parents to enhance their children clearly frightens many prominent policy intellectuals on both the political Left and the Right.

The godfather of the antibiotech left is activist Jeremy Rifkin and his Foundation on Economic Trends. He is now ably assisted by environmentalist Bill McKibben. Also arguing against biotech from the left is George Annas, who proposes a global ban on reproductive cloning and all interventions in the human germline, including those aimed at curing genetic diseases.

But objections to biotech cross traditional political boundaries. As we've seen fighting against bioprogress from the right we have, most prominently, Leon Kass, head of the President's Council on Bioethics. He is joined by such leading conservative intellectuals as *Weekly Standard* editor William Kristol and Francis Fukuyama.

Fear of Future Possibilities

When grappling with the fears and anxieties of biotechnophobes, we should remember that we are still in many ways arguing about potentialities, not current realities. Enabling parents to genetically enhance their children is not going to be as easy as some of us might hope, nor will it happen as soon as we might wish. Right now nascent genetic enhancement technologies are simply not safe enough for use. Any future enhancement technologies will have to be thoroughly tested in animals before they can be used to help people.

Fortunately, our quickly advancing understanding of the complex web of interactions between genes and other cellular activities is likely to dramatically reduce the risks that might accompany inserting beneficial genes. A good general benchmark is that attempts at genetic enhancement should be delayed until solid research indicates that the risk of birth defects using such technologies is at least no greater than the risks of birth defects in children produced conventionally.

However, even those who fear their arrival agree that safe genetic enhancements are just over the horizon. Bioconservatives on both the Left and the Right fear that future biotechnological progress will transform humanity so much that our descendants will become, as Fukuyama says, "posthuman." They regularly invoke the dystopian visions of Mary Shelley's *Frankenstein*, Aldous Huxley's *Brave New World*, and C.S. Lewis's *The Abolition of Man* as warnings of what a future of unleashed human biotechnology might hold. Fortunately, they are wrong.

Individuality Is Not Based Solely on Genes

Many opponents of human genetic engineering are either conscious or unconscious genetic determinists. They fear that the advance of biotechnological knowledge and practice will somehow undermine human freedom. In a sense, these genetic determinists believe that human freedom resides in the gaps of our knowledge of our genetic makeup. Typical in this regard is McKibben. Like other bioconservatives, McKibben accepts that the fondest dreams of the proponents of human genetic engineering eventually could come to pass. He even admits that advanced biomedical science could someday spare children from congenital diseases, cure cancers, correct disabilities, and lengthen the human life span.

Most people would embrace these possibilities with optimism, even joy. But for McKibben, these seeming advantages spell a dismal future for mankind. Parents who choose to use genetic engineering will end up turning their children into "robots" and "automatons." "Down that path," he declared in a recent debate, "lies the death of what we call human meaning, the idea that people are in some way their own human beings and are not pre-programmed semi-robots."

Human freedom, McKibben evidently believes, depends in some profound sense on the random inheritance of the genes that are the recipes for our bodies and brains. As a result of this random genetic inheritance, he suggests, we have greater scope for freedom than if our genes had been chosen for us. McKibben is indulging in genetic essentialism: the unwarranted idea that we are just meat puppets dangling from our strands of DNA.

McKibben is obviously right when he declares, "*[G]enes do matter.*" But they don't matter as much as McKibben thinks they do. Take the case of monozygotic twins who share exactly the same genes and were formed in the same womb at the same time. They are certainly not identical people. In fact, variance between traits such as intelligence, personality, and even weight correlate only 60 to 70 percent between identical twins. That's much closer than with nonidentical siblings, but it's still a wide variance.

The case of identical twins proves the point that it is our brains, and not our genes, that make us individual human beings. That's why, in recent years, our society has legally defined death as brain death. Once our brains are gone, we are gone, even though our bodies—with all their genes—may live on. The fact is that we respect people, not their genomes. In a very real sense, we are no longer at the mercy of genes. Our genes are now at the mercy of our brains.

Biology also increasingly reveals that human individuality doesn't depend just on having different genes; it is the result of the interplay between genes and environment. A gene that enhances one's capacity for music doesn't mean that its possessor must become another Wolfgang Amadeus Mozart or, Mick Jagger. Genes simply don't work that way. All of us have many capacities stemming from his or her specific genetic endowment. Perhaps I could have become a professional basketball player or a computer engineer, but I chose not to develop those particular abilities, despite the fact that my specific complement of genes might have allowed me to do so.

Genes order the production of different proteins in response to environmental influences such as schooling, physical training, infections, and nutrition. For example, as we learn, the genes in brain cells produce new proteins to fix memories and strengthen connections between nerves. Human genes are the necessary recipes for making human brains and bodies, but brains and bodies are manifestly shaped by their experiences. It might be possible someday, using genetic engineering, to give a child a brain smart enough to understand mathematician Andrew Wiles's proof of Fermat's Last Theorem. But she will have to undergo the experience of learning mathematics first. There are no genes for specific math problems.

Ignorance Is Not Freedom

Human freedom cannot and does not rely on ignorance and randomness. Human freedom—the capacity to make choices based on reason—expands with knowledge. If you don't believe it, think about how humanity's greater knowledge of such things as the germ theory of disease and the atomic theory of matter have radically increased humankind's choices and freedom during the last two centuries. Most of us would agree that there has certainly been an improvement over our ancestors' world—a world filled with friendly and hostile animistic spirits, one in which half of all children died before their first birthday.

Similarly, knowledge about how our genes affect our behavior and how our brains are wired increases rather than limits our freedom. Prozac, for example, does not limit our choices; it gives depressed people the freedom to adjust their emotional state. Ignorance is not freedom. Knowledge is freedom; ignorance is slavery.

In any case, if McKibben really believes that human freedom depends on inheriting a random selection of genes, his cause is already lost. Why? Genetic testing. Even McKibben recognizes that such testing will soon be here. "The biotech pioneer Craig Venter said in 2002 that within five years a personalized printout of an individual's genetic code would be cheap enough for anyone to buy, so you'll probably be able to afford it late next week or so," he writes. In fact, in 2002 Venter offered to scan an individual's entire genome in a week for only $712,000. Genetic testing will enable every one of us to know precisely our entire complement of randomly acquired genes. The good news is that we will then know our predispositions to various diseases, enabling us to take steps to delay their onset or even prevent them altogether.

To McKibben, such knowledge is a blow to our freedom, because we will also know a lot more about how our particular sets of genes influence our temperaments, our intelligence, our memories, and our physical capacities. Of course, that knowledge may well expand our freedom and our choices by making it possible for us to intervene by means of pharmaceuticals and optimized training to change our temperaments, improve our memories, or strengthen our bodies. Human freedom will then properly be seen as residing, at least partially, in our ability to overcome these predispositions, much as a former alcoholic can overcome his thirst for booze or an overweight person can lose weight by dieting.

McKibben's fears that genetic engineering will reduce human freedom are misplaced. To the extent that genes "program" us, we are already "preprogrammed" by our randomly conferred genes; we are just ignorant about which ones are doing what programming. But that won't be the case in the near future.

Genetic Enhancement Will Lead to Greater Freedom

Providing children with such enhanced capacities as good health, stronger bodies, and cleverer brains, far from turning them into robots will give them greater freedom and more choices. Almost everyone would want to have these beneficial traits. Those of us who regard a poor immune system, a weaker body, or an IQ of 80 as privations will welcome the opportunity to help our children avoid such conditions, even as we try now to keep our children safe and healthy, and to inspire and educate them.

McKibben objects that future gene-enhanced children will not have consented to receiving the genes selected by their parents. "The person left without any choice *at all* is the one you've engineered," he asserts. "You've decided, for once and for all, certain things about him: he'll have genes expressing proteins that send extra dopamine to alter his mood; he'll have genes expressing proteins to boost his memory; to shape his stature."

To the extent that this is true, it is true for unengineered kids now. It's just that parents don't know which genes they've conferred on their children. Of course, they hope for the best—that their kids got the genes for good health, strong bodies, and sound brains. But there's always a chance they ended up with Grandma's genes for early heart disease or those that led to Uncle Jim's schizophrenia. Genetic engineering will help parents in the future avoid some of those harmful outcomes.

McKibben is correct that a gene-engineered child would have no choice about whether to express the proteins that lead to early onset Alzheimer's disease. But it's a pretty good bet that kids won't regret the parents' decision to eliminate those deleterious genes. But before we unthinkingly accept McKibben's misleading concerns about a child's informed consent, we should keep firmly in mind that *not one of us now living was asked our consent to be born, much less to be born with the complement of randomly conferred genes that we carry.*

Let's say a parent could choose genes that would guarantee her child a 20-point IQ boost. It is reasonable to presume that the child would be happy to consent to this enhancement of her capacities. How about plugging in genes that would boost her immune system and guarantee that she would never get colon cancer, Alzheimer's, AIDS, or the common cold? Again, it seems reasonable to assume consent. These enhancements are general capacities that any human being would reasonably want to have. In fact, lots of children already have these capacities naturally, so it's hard to see any moral justification for outlawing access to them for others.

Instead of submitting to the tyranny of nature's lottery, which cruelly deals out futures blighted with ill health, stunted mental abilities, and early death, parents would be able to open more possibilities for their children to lead fulfilling lives. Genetic enhancements to prevent these ills would not violate a child's liberty or autonomy, and certainly do not constitute a form of genetic slavery, as some opponents claim. Giving children such enhanced capacities as good health, stronger bodies, and cleverer brains, far from constraining them, would in fact give them greater freedom and more choices.

It's surely a strange kind of despotism that enlarges a person's abilities and options in life. In fact, through the gift of technology conjured from human intelligence, parents can increasingly bestow not only the gift of life, but also the gift of good health on their children. The good news is that any would-be tyrannical parents who buy into the bioconservatives' erroneous notions of hard genetic determinism will be disappointed. Their children will have minds and inclinations distinctly their own, albeit genetically enhanced. . . .

Questions of Equality

McKibben has more specifically political concerns about bioengineering. He fears it will exacerbate inequality, even as he worries about homogenization. In his first scenario, the rich get access to safe genetic enhancements first, dramatically widening the gap between the rich and the poor. "The political equality enshrined in the Declaration of Independence can't withstand the destruction of the idea that humans are in fact equal," writes McKibben. He is citing a similar worry expressed by Fukuyama. who declares. "The political equality enshrined in the Declaration of Independence rests on the empirical fact of natural human equality." Marcy Darnovsky, associate executive director of the left-wing Center for Genetics and Society in Oakland, California, argues that supporters of biotechnological progress will violate the most sacred tenets of American democracy by "inscrib[ing] inequality onto the human genome."

But are people "in fact equal"? There is nothing at all self-evident about physical human equality or equality of status. Some people are short, some tall; some fat, others thin; some strong, others weak; some poor, others rich; some brilliant, others dim. In other words, what we see is not self-evident equality, but human diversity and human individuality.

The ideal of political equality arose from the Enlightenment insistence that since no one has access to absolute truth, no one has a moral right to impose his or her values and beliefs on others. Political equality has never rested on claims about human biology. We all had the same human biology during the long millennia in which slavery, purdah [confinement], patriarchy, and aristocratic rule were social norms. Over the last two hundred years, human biology didn't change—our politics did.

The modern ideals of democracy and political equality are sustained chiefly by the insight, developed by Enlightenment thinkers, that people are responsible moral agents who can distinguish right from wrong, and therefore deserve equal consideration before the law and a respected place in our political community. The broad ability to distinguish right from wrong does not depend on the genetics of IQ, skin color, or gender. With respect to political equality, genetic differences are already differences that make no difference. Having some

133

citizens who take advantage of genetic technologies and others who do not won't alter that principle.

Bioconservatives on both the Left and the Right also worry that genetic engineering will create two warring classes in society—the enhanced versus the naturals. Left-leaning bioethicists George Annas, Lori Andrews, and Rosario Isasi are brutally blunt about their fears of conflict between the genetically enhanced and unenhanced: "The new species, or 'posthuman,' will likely view the old 'normal' humans as inferior, even savages, and fit for slavery or slaughter. The normals, on the other hand, may see the posthumans as a threat and if they can, may engage in a preemptive strike by killing the posthumans before they themselves are killed or enslaved by them. It is ultimately this predictable potential for genocide that makes species-altering experiments potential weapons of mass destruction, and makes the unaccountable genetic engineer a potential bioterrorist."

Another crowning achievement of the Enlightenment is the principle of tolerance, of putting up with people who look different, talk differently, worship differently, and live differently than we do. In the future, our descendants may not all be "natural" *Homo sapiens*. But they will still be moral beings who can be held accountable for their actions. Political liberalism is already the answer to bioconservative concerns about human and posthuman rights and interactions. In liberal societies the law is meant to apply equally to all, no matter how rich or poor, powerful or powerless, brilliant or stupid, enhanced or unenhanced. There is no reason to think that the same liberal political and moral principles that apply to diverse human beings today wouldn't apply to relations among future humans and posthumans. . . .

Genetic Enhancement Would Not Reduce People's Humanity

Taking McKibben's concerns about our vanishing humanity seriously, if, for example, genetic engineering changes the range of typical human emotions, wouldn't that change what it means to be human? After all, no parents would want to give their children genes for emotional depression or a violent temper. University of Maryland's Institute for Philosophy and Public Policy senior research scholar Marc Sagoff claims that in order to qualify as being human, one must possess the emotional capacities that are characteristic of our species. Manipulating the human genome in a way that alters these capacities threatens the concept of human beings. If biotechnological manipulations removed our ability to feel anger, hate, or violence, "we would in an important sense not be human beings," argues Sagoff. We'd still be members of the species *Homo sapiens* and we would still be moral beings, but not human beings as understood in previous ages.

But let's say that future genetic engineers discover that there is a gene that predisposes carriers to suicidal depression and that they can fix it. Would fixing it make subsequent generations nonhuman beings? After all, most people today do not fall into suicidal depressions, and those happy people are no less human than, say, the famously suicidal poet Sylvia Plath. Besides, depression can already be ameliorated for many people by means of Prozac or Paxil. Surely, taking serotonin reuptake inhibitors does not make people other or less than human. Sufferers of depression will tell you that the drugs do not make them feel less human; instead, they claim the drugs restore them to their true selves.

Most of us may already be incapable of berserker rage or religious ecstasy. Yet we are fully human beings, too. Sagoff cannot morally argue that parents must be forbidden to eliminate genes that predispose their offspring to suicidal depression on the grounds that that will deprive the rest of us of a sufficient number of great novelists in the future. . . .

Bioconservatives often accuse biotechnological progressives who would allow access to safe genetic enhancements of not being "worried about diminishing the sanctity of human life."

But who really has a higher regard for the sanctity of human life—those who, like Kass and McKibben, fatalistically counsel us to live with the often bum hands that nature deals us, or those who want to use genetic technologies to ameliorate the ills that have afflicted humanity since time immemorial? Respecting the sanctity of life doesn't require that we take whatever random horrors nature dishes out. Safe genetic engineering, when it becomes possible, strongly affirms the intrinsic value of human life by producing healthier, stronger, smarter people more equipped to enjoy their lives and to thrive during them.

No matter how advanced, technologies—including genetic enhancement—are not ends in themselves. They are means for individuals to build the best lives they can for themselves and their families. The decisions to use them or not are personal questions. These private arenas should not be open to public decision making. For a man who says he favors human freedom and choice, McKibben seems awfully eager to limit both. . . .

Grateful Future Generations

What horrors do . . . designer babies face? Longer, healthier, smarter, and perhaps even happier lives? It is hard to see any ethical problem with that. It is true for genetic engineering, as for all other technologies, that some people will misuse it; tragedies will occur. Given the sorry history of government-sponsored eugenics, it is vital that control over genetic engineering never be given to any governmental authority. But to use biotechnology and genetic engineering is not, by definition, to abuse it. This technology offers the prospect of ever-greater freedom for people, and should be welcomed by everyone who cares about human happiness and human flourishing.

Oxford University bioethicist Julian Savulescu is right when he reminds us, "The Nazis sought to interfere directly in people's reproductive decisions (by forcing them to be sterilized) to promote social ideals, particularly around racial superiority. Not offering selection for nondisease genes would indirectly interfere (by denying choice) to promote social ideals such as equality or 'population welfare.' There is no relevant difference between direct and indirect eugenics. The lesson we learned from eugenics is that society should be loath to interfere (directly and indirectly) in reproductive decision-making."

People who benefit from the fruits of biotechnological progress in the future will be neither Frankenstein's monsters nor genetic robots. Rather, they will be our grateful descendants for whom we have eased the burdens of disease, disability, and early death—if only we choose not to slow or kill the development of this new technology. They will look back in wonder, and perhaps in horror, at those who would have denied them the blessings of biomedical progress.

Genetic Enhancement Is Ethical for Adults but Not for Children

David Plotz

David Plotz is deputy editor of the online magazine Slate. *In the following selection he describes the major objections of those who oppose genetic enhancement of humans, and he argues that they are not valid except in reference to children. In his opinion, it is not wrong for adults to enhance themselves in ways that do not alter the DNA passed on to their offspring, but they should not enhance their children. He states that changing the genes of embryos is too risky and may result in children that do not come out the way their parents expect. Parents, he says, have always had unreasonable expectations for their children, but genetic enhancement represents a new and particularly dangerous form of those expectations.*

Is enhancement a good idea? Is it right (and—a separate question—is it wise?) to give yourself infrared vision or a turbo-memory or MGF [Mechano Growth Formula]-pumped muscles? There is a range of ways to approach these questions.

Would-be enhancers—a category that includes scientists, gung-ho sci-fi fans, muscleheads, longevity nuts, etc.—use two strategies to dismiss ethical questions as irrelevant. First, they claim the coming enhancements are nothing new: We have always enhanced ourselves. As Carl Elliott—*not* an enhancement advocate, I should say in his defense—points out in his new book *Better Than Well*, yesterday's enhancement is today's necessity. When Elliott was a boy, such mundane activities as removing warts, medicating acne, and immunizing kids counted as enhancements: They allowed people to improve what had been the inevitable human condition. Glasses, contact lenses, and laser surgery all improve on nature's work, but you don't hear anyone agonizing over them. The supporters of enhancement suggest that tomorrow's improvements are no different. In a generation, we will feel the same way about MGF-buffed pectorals as about nose jobs.

This argument doesn't persuade me. Today's enhancers have extraordinarily grand ambitions, much greater than zapping warts or enlarging breasts. They crave powers that have been reserved for gods (superhuman strength) or beasts (infrared night vision). They also seek to change human beings permanently—something no previous enhancer could do. Doctors will soon be able to swap genes in and out of embryos, protecting children from diseases or perhaps increasing intelligence or adding height. Such "germline engineering" will irrevocably alter the DNA of those kids and of the species. Clearasil, it ain't.

The second argument for enhancement is its inevitability: Consumer demand drives enhancement, so it will happen if people want it, whatever the ethics might be. Just consider the history of cosmetic surgery: Who would honestly claim medical justification for breast implants and nose jobs? But consumers wanted ski-jump noses, and they got ski-jump noses. The same market ruthlessness applies to tomorrow's enhancements.

Such shrugging is also unsatisfactory. Government legislation, moral suasion, journalistic haranguing, and medical self-policing still have huge influence on what kind of enhancements do and don't succeed. The market may make it inevitable that athletes will use EPO [erythropoietin, an agent that increases production of red blood cells], or that students will take Provigil [a stimulant], but that does not answer the question of whether they are right to do so.

Those who oppose enhancement have four major objections:

Safety

Every few weeks a story breaks about another gene therapy trial gone awry. A teenager dies in Pennsylvania. Two toddlers develop leukemia in France. These mishaps are tolerated because the subjects in question would have died without gene therapy in any case. In theory, medicine will tolerate terrible risks to save lives or repair disabilities but not to make patients feel better about themselves. This is the essence of the "therapy/enhancement" distinction favored by medical ethicists.

But the distinction between therapy and enhancement isn't as clear as ethicists contend. Doctors practice enhancement all the time—even frivolous enhancement. Surgeons undoubtedly claim that there's a therapeutic justification for breast enlargements, but they're not kidding anyone.

What's more, a recent revolution in patient expectations has further blurred the cultural value we place on this distinction. In the past generation, doctors have become less authoritarian, and patients better-informed about their condition and the risks and benefits they face. (The Internet and books such as Sherwin Nuland's seminal *How We Die* have particularly galvanized patients.) The sanctity of doctor-knows-best has been diluted as doctors increasingly accept that a patient can make his own choices, including the choice to take physical risks for the sake of self-improvement.

There is also an obvious libertarian counterargument to the safety problem: We allow adults to take all kinds of risks for the sake of pleasure—from jumping cars on motorcycles to piercing their nipples to humiliating themselves on *Joe Millionaire*. Enhancement is no different, except it usually requires a doctor's help. It's my body, and I'll pry if I want to.

But the libertarian argument fades when it comes to enhancing children. Currently, we permit parents to accept medical risks on behalf of their children but only for physical problems. The government should discourage, and perhaps even prevent, parents from exposing their children to terrible risks for the sake of ambition. It's wrong for parents to risk a kid's eyesight for supervision or dose their promising young linebacker with MGF so he can win a scholarship to Notre Dame.

Cheating

A few weeks ago, I heard [bioethicist] Leon Kass lecture on the perils of enhancement. After much eloquent agonizing, he concluded that enhancement is troubling because it's a form of cheating. His was a Protestant ethic critique. Enhancement allows us to gain extraordinary powers without working for them, severing the "relationship between doing and accomplishment." This cheating diminishes us by depriving us of the sense that we must work to make anything worthwhile.

But the logical conclusion of Kass' argument against enhancement is that things were much better in the Bronze Age. After all, the last several thousand years have been an endless march toward diminishing the amount of drudge work we have to do. The automobile cheats us of the work of walking to our destination. Anesthetics deprive women of the healthy pain they should feel during childbirth. Computers weaken our brains by performing the computations that we should be doing in our heads. Yet we've embraced automobile and computers; why should his argument stand only when it comes to enhancement?

There is a fundamental weakness to the cheating argument: Enhancements do not eliminate work. They just change the nature of it. For example, football players train much harder today than they did a generation ago, even though many of them cheat with steroids. They play a game that is faster and more physical (and better) than it used to be. Why is the game better? The players are faster and stronger and better-conditioned—in part because they cheat with steroids. Similarly, computers have not abolished work: They have liberated people to explore new, different subjects, rather than waste their time adding columns of numbers or endlessly retyping documents.

Hubris

Evolution is a slow and fussy process. Human beings have taken shape over millions of years. There have been false starts, countless mutations, blind alleys. But the enhancers propose radically altering our genes in an evolutionary blink of an eye. They want to start adding DNA to embryos and manufacturing new genes to insert in our eyes and ears and muscles.

This is unsettling. Can the brain and body handle such extraordinary shake-ups? For the moment, we are very crude workmen with DNA. Genetic enhancement may be a wonderful future prospect, but we shouldn't play with it casually. We may create genes that we can't control, engineer children who don't come out the way we expect.

Equality

The rich will be enhanced first. Only folks with cash to burn will be able to afford the fancy new memory drugs or fiendishly complicated new gene transfer technologies.

This is troubling for two reasons. First, frivolous enhancement siphons away resources from basic health care for billions. (Then again, so does Viagra, or research on balding, or liposuction.)

Second, is it right to let the enhanced group exploit their advantage to rule over the rest of us? The rich kid can score the Provigil that keeps him alert through the SAT, but the poor kid can't. The job applicant who takes memory drugs will have the jump on one who doesn't. The inequities could be glaring.

But people already gain all kinds of unfair advantages from being tall or white or good-looking or rich. Enhancement is, in some ways, a less troubling kind of inequity because it has something to do with actual ability. The person who takes the memory drug probably *can* do a better job at the law firm than the person who doesn't. The enhancement really will help performance (unlike good looks, which wouldn't make someone a better lawyer).

Moreover, we should be so lucky that our societal problems concern people who are overqualified and hypertalented. It may be, in some sense, unfair to create a class of enhanced people, but that does not mean that it is *wrong* to do so. If enhancements do work, perhaps they ought not be banned or restricted to prevent inequality but made more readily available. We ought to want more of them, not fewer.

My own views on the ethics of enhancement are situational. It depends on the kind of enhancement and the age of the person who wants it. I share the "Hubris" concern about all germline engineering. We don't know what damage we may do when we permanently change the human genome. One day, germline engineering could be a miracle for mankind. But before we would know it is safe, many babies would be put at risk, and some would almost certainly suffer and die.

As for enhancements that don't permanently amend DNA, I'm enough of a libertarian that I don't see any reason to stop adults from altering their bodies to suit themselves. If they want to take pills or add weird implants or even temporarily change genes with somatic therapy, good luck to them. They have nothing to lose but their brains.

But I don't feel the same way about enhancing kids. Parents always have unreasonable expectations for their children—*you'll never go to medical school with those grades, young man*—but enhancements represent a new and particularly dangerous form of those expectations. Don't tinker with your child to further your own ambitions. Tinker with yourself instead.

Genetic Enhancement of Athletes Might Harm Sports

Gregory M. Lamb

Gregory M. Lamb is a staff writer at the Christian Science Monitor, *a major newspaper. In the following selection, he reports on the worry that is developing over the possibility that athletes will seek genetic enhancement to acquire competitive advantage. The World Anti-Doping Agency (WADA) has already declared such enhancement—or gene doping—illegal. Some bioethicists, however, say that the practice should be regulated, not banned, in sports, both because gene enhancement would have legitimate use in recovery from sports injuries and because a ban would drive the practice underground. Not enough is yet known about the potential side effects of genetic enhancement to judge what is safe to try. However, Lamb says, the benefits will be overwhelmingly attractive to athletes and some experts believe that legalizing it would turn sports into a freak show.*

It would make today's "cat and mouse" detection of drug-taking athletes seem trivial. It would produce excellence without effort, challenging the spirit of the Olympics and the meaning of all sports competition. More broadly, it could become a kind of referendum on how the world views the improvement of humans through technology.

The catalyst is an emerging science called gene modification or gene enhancement. Using it, an athlete could be injected with the DNA of an animal, for example, and quickly become much faster and stronger. "You don't need to lift weights, and you don't need to go on 10-mile runs to train for endurance," explains Peter Weyand, who teaches kinesiology—the study of muscles and human movement—at Rice University in Houston. "It would replace training; it would make training seem trivial and more than obsolete. Somebody who's not athletic at all could be transformed into something superhuman."

Today's world-class athletes are already genetic oddities, possessing superior native abilities that they hone through training—and in some cases, through illegal drugs. But with genetic engineering, anyone might enhance his or her abilities "100, 200, 500, 1,000 percent," Dr. Weyand says. Borrowing the fast-twitch muscles of a mouse, for example, could create superfast sprinters. "If you start to think about the extremes in nature, it's absolutely frightening" to consider what's possible, he adds.

The World Anti-Doping Agency (WADA), which determines which substances are banned in international sports competitions, is so concerned that it has already declared gene doping illegal, even though it believes it's unlikely that anyone is doing it yet. "The time to grab hold of this matter is now," said Richard Pound, president of WADA, at a meeting of prominent scientists earlier this year [2004]. He urged them to devise ways to detect genetic enhancement even as they develop the technique. Medical researchers are excited about the possibilities of genetic therapies to help patients with muscle diseases such as muscular dystrophy, and to strengthen the elderly.

Genetic Enhancement of Rats Increases Strength

Interest in genetic enhancement in the sports world has exploded since publication in March [2004] of a study in a scientific journal showing that mice and rats underwent remarkable changes when injected with a gene that promotes growth. H. Lee Sweeney, a University of Pennsylvania researcher, found that these "Schwarzenegger mice" showed up to 50 percent muscle growth. Rats altered in the same way gained 35 percent in strength when the technique was combined with exercise. Since reporting his findings, Dr. Sweeney has been inundated with requests for information from coaches and athletes.

Though Sweeney's work is years away from trials in humans, that doesn't mean that others might not be quietly moving ahead, eager to reap the benefits. "The technology is available now for athletes to use. They're taking a big risk by doing it, but nevertheless it's out there, and they could be trying it," says Andy Miah, a bioethicist whose book *Genetically Modified Athletes: Biomedical Ethics, Gene Doping and Sport*, was published last month [July 2004] in Britain. As last year's sports scandal over the designer steroid THG and the continuing drug disqualifications at this year's Olympics show, "athletes are still doing things we don't know about," he says.

Gene therapies hold so much promise for helping humanity, Dr. Miah says, that he has urged the WADA not to treat them simply as a new form of illegal doping. For example, gene therapy potentially could be used to repair the injured muscles of athletes. Would that use also be illegal? "It's that kind of boundary that's unclear from the present rulings," he says. By making genetic modification illegal, athletes may seek out "rogue scientists," he says. "If we do prohibit it, we push it underground, and we don't know what athletes are doing. They don't know what they're doing." If we regulate instead, "we can try to make sure they're doing it in a safe manner," he says.

That's why Miah favors legalization and regulation over a ban. The world of sports already recognizes differences in innate ability, he says, as shown by the paralympics competition for those with various disabilities, and the use of weight classes in sports such as boxing. Regulation would make it possible to look at the genetic profiles of athletes and decide which ones are suited to compete against one another, he says.

Side Effects of Genetic Enhancement Are Unknown

Right now, no test exists to detect genetic enhancement,

Today's world-class athletes possess superior abilities that many fear could be secretly enhanced through genetic modification. © Corel Corporation

though finding foreign DNA eventually might be possible by taking tissue samples from athletes. Equally unknown are the side effects.

"All bets are off when you start playing with genetic engi neering ... in terms of system function, organ function, and long-term effects," says Weyand. "If you put in superfast muscle, are you going to alter function in a way that the tendons and the bones might not be able to support the loads? ... You might start to snap tendons and bones. There might be deleterious health effects. We really don't know."

Yet the benefits will be overwhelmingly attractive to athletes. Strength and speed aren't the only abilities that could be supersized. Red blood cells could be enhanced to carry more oxygen, revolutionizing endurance sports such as cycling, cross-country skiing, and long-distance running. The technique also might be used to alter the way athletes sense pain, Miah says, allowing them to push themselves harder and challenging sports' ancient work ethic: "No pain, no gain."

"It's a terrible situation," says John Hoberman, a professor at the University of Texas at Austin who has studied the history of sports doping. Legalizing genetic modification would lead to "anarchy," he says. "Inevitably it's going to turn [sports] into a kind of circus—a freak show."

Development of Genetic Enhancement Technologies Is Inevitable

Françoise Baylis and Jason Scott Robert

Françoise Baylis is a professor of bioethics and philosophy at Dalhousie University in Canada. Jason Scott Robert is a professor of bioethics and philosophy at Arizona State University. In the following selection these two authors argue that future development and use of genetic enhancement technologies is inevitable. They present several reasons for this opinion: such technologies will be commercially profitable; if free choice is not restricted, these technologies will be developed; human curiosity will lead to their pursuit; competition will promote them; and humans are now thought to be capable of directing the course of evolution. They conclude that genetic enhancement is humanity's destiny.

According to some, genetic enhancement technologies are inevitable—and welcome—because they promise to secure health, success, wealth and happiness, especially for the presently disadvantaged. [Geneticist] James Watson holds such a view, as does [bioethicist] Gregory Stock, but despite its popularity this hypothesis surely strains one's credulity. Ours is not a kind, caring, compassionate world, but rather a capitalist, heedlessly liberal, curiosity-driven, competition-infused world in which some are intent on controlling the human evolutionary story.

Biotechnology Will Be Developed for Commercial Reasons

Genetic enhancement technologies are inevitable because so many of us are crass capitalists, eager to embrace biocapital-

ism. In economically advanced industrialised countries, ours is a corporate world where there is a shared commitment to capitalism, privatisation, and a market-driven global economy. In this world, marked by globalisation, free markets, and consumer choice, there is no enhancement technology that is too dangerous, or too transgressive, for it not to be pursued. Unrestrained consumerism is good and if this results in a free-market eugenic meritocracy, so be it.

In this worldview, only commercial viability (marketability and profitability) matters. If a genetic enhancement technology can be developed and sold (at a profit), it will be made and marketed (and not necessarily in that order). Particular nation-states can try to prohibit the development of the technology, but ultimately are unlikely to be successful. One reason, explored by [psychiatrist William] Gardner, is that once any nation-state endorses human genetic enhancement as a way to gain an industrial-commercial edge, other nation-states will be forced to follow suit. A second reason concerns not nation-states but multinational corporations. The state's authority and power have been seriously eroded by globalisation. Multinationals are widely recognised as more powerful than elected governments and thus, not surprisingly, their commercial interests prevail. Whether at the level of nation-states or multinational industries, ethical concerns are easily swept aside when there is (serious) money to be made.

This mercantile account of the modern world is critically incomplete, however—not least because very many of us aim to transcend crass capitalism. So, eagerness to embrace biocapitalism cannot completely explain the inevitability of genetic enhancement technologies.

Free Choice Will Lead to Biotechnology

Genetic enhancement technologies are inevitable because heedless liberalism is rampant. [Bioethicist] Leon Kass observes that prohibitionists are struggling 'against the general liberal prejudice that it is wrong to stop people doing something.' [Bioethicist] Jeffrey Kahn similarly notes the (perhaps uniquely) American reticence to prohibit certain types of research and development because of the prevailing attitude that 'capitalistic acts between consenting adults are none of its business.' Within states, the liberal reduction of the ethical complexities of genetic enhancement technologies to the sacred paradigm of individual free choice virtually guarantees the inevitability of the technologies; meanwhile, more globally, the liberal reluctance to move beyond this paradigm engenders a more general attitude of cultural relativism whereby there is neither the imperative nor the opportunity to deem some activities as just plain wrong.

Such a political diagnosis of the modern world is also seriously incomplete, however—not least because it invokes an unfair caricature of liberalism and fails to appreciate the complexities of political life both nationally and globally. So heedless liberalism is also unable to completely account for the inevitability of genetic enhancement technologies.

Human Curiosity Will Lead to Biotechnology

Genetic enhancement technologies are inevitable because humans are naturally inquisitive (and tinkering) beings. Ours is a curiosity-driven, knowledge-based world that is fascinated with technology and in which the guiding mantra is 'if it can be done, it will be done, and so we should do it first.' In this world, the quest for knowledge for knowledge's sake is an all-consuming passion; understanding ourselves, unravelling the mystery of our existence, is our Holy Grail. Add to this our love of technology, and the inevitability of embracing genetic enhancement technology becomes evident. With research on genetic manipulation there is the prospect 'to improve our understanding of the most complex and compelling phenomenon ever observed—the life process. We cannot be expected to deny ourselves this knowledge.' Nor can we be expected to restrain ourselves from harnessing and applying this knowledge.

A key feature of this worldview is the belief that scientific knowledge is value-free and yet immensely valuable. Consider the following two recent statements:

> Scientists liberate truth from prejudice, and through their work lend wings to society's aspirations. While poetry titillates and theology obfuscates, science liberates. . . . Science, with its currently successful pursuit of universal competence, should be acknowledged king. [Chemistry professor Peter Atkins]

> Reliable scientific knowledge has no moral or ethical value. . . . Science tells us how the world is. . . . Danger and ethical issues come into play when scientific research is done in practice, for example in experiments involving humans and other animals, or when science is applied to technology, or in issues related to safety. There is thus an important distinction between science and technology: between knowledge and understanding on the one hand, and the application of that knowledge to making something, or using it in some practical way, on the other. [Biology professor Lewis Wolpert]

In this view, while knowledge can be used to pursue less than praiseworthy technological interventions, this is not sufficient reason to halt the quest for scientific knowledge and understanding. If there are concerns about the misuse of knowledge in the development of a particular technology, then these should appropriately be directed to the eventual application of the technology, not hinder the search for purest scientific knowledge.

Again, some would argue that this view of the world is seriously flawed, not least because scientific knowledge, like all knowledge, is value-laden. Moreover, the distinction between (basic) scientific knowledge and (applied) technology does not withstand critical scrutiny. While some would want to restrict or forbid genetic engineering in humans, it must be remembered 'that it would be difficult to separate . . . knowledge of molecular genetics from the know-how that manipulates the chromosome.'

This account of the inevitability of genetic enhancement technologies is therefore also incomplete, as the pursuit of knowledge is bound up with social and political (and economic) factors. A worldview according to which knowledge is neutral and can be sought for its own sake, is impoverished and so cannot completely explain the inevitability of genetic enhancement technologies.

Competition Will Lead to Biotechnology

Genetic enhancement technologies are inevitable because humans are competitive beings, always looking for new and challenging opportunities to maximise personal, social and economic advantage. Competition is (and has been) a valued human activity not only in itself but also instrumentally— competition promotes the drive to succeed and thus fosters improvement. In work, in sport, in reproduction (and in other contexts as well), competition is both encouraged and rewarded. Humans have, throughout the ages, repeatedly shown themselves to be competitive beings driven to succeed (and/or to exceed), and willing to use most any means available to achieve the desired end.

In this view, there can be no doubt that genetic enhancement technologies will be among the means used to secure competitive or positional advantage. To be sure, this use of genetic enhancement technologies may be unfair (as when the genetic enhancements are available only to a small elite) or it may be self-defeating (as when the genetic enhancements are universally available and electively used by all so that no relative advantage is gained). No matter. The point remains that genetic enhancement technologies will be used (by some or all) in attempts to gain a competitive advantage either by strengthening a particular capacity needed to pursue a specific life goal (increased height for the aspiring basketball player, or increased dexterity for the budding pianist), or by strengthening a range of capacities likely to increase one's ability to effectively pursue and master a range of options.

This worldview is flawed, however, in its narrow account of the human drive to compete and succeed. As [philosopher] Dan Brock astutely notes, and as we make clear above regarding means mattering morally, 'sometimes a valued human activity is defined in part by the means it employs, not just by the ends at which it aims.' While competition is a valued human activity, this is, in large measure, because of the way it engages our physical, intellectual and other capacities. For many of us it is not only about winning, but also about how the game is played. In large part this explains the ban on the use of performance enhancement drugs in Olympic competition. In this view, achieving success in the workplace or elsewhere by means of genetic enhancement would hardly be worth the candle. As such, our competitive spirit alone cannot account for the inevitability of genetic enhancement technologies.

In sum, a common flaw with each of these characterisations of the modern world—characterisations of worldviews—is that they are one-dimensional: based either in simplistic economic, political, scientific, or sociological terms. The inevitability of genetic enhancement technologies demands a more encompassing, multi-dimensional diagnosis.

Humans Can Direct the Course of Evolution

Genetic enhancement technologies are inevitable because the future is ours for the shaping. Ours is a dynamic world in which change is a constant, characterised historically by a variety of cultural revolutions (in language development, agriculture, political organisation, physical technologies and, now, biotechnologies), each of which has significantly shaped the human species. Given the economic, political, scientific, and sociological realities sketched above, some firmly believe that the time has come for humans to shape our own destiny and to direct the course of evolution. Genetic enhancement technologies are seen as our most powerful tool for this purpose.

In previous times, humans saw themselves as beings created in the image of a divine God, later as products of natural selection, and more recently as bundles of selfish genes shaped by selection. Now some see humans as self-transforming beings capable of, and intent on, refashioning ourselves in our own image of what we should be. In this worldview there are and should be no restrictions—financial, moral, epistemic, biological—on what is possible.

This worldview would appear to rest on a particular understanding of human purpose. Following [psychologist Abraham] Maslow, what distinguishes humans is the drive toward self-actualisation—the desire to realise human potentialities. For generations, increasing percentages of the population in many countries have not had to strive to meet lower-order physiological and safety needs. A direct consequence of this is that some humans have been able to direct their energies to the pursuit of higher order needs, the ultimate goal being to satisfy their desire to realise themselves to the fullest. These individuals have tested their physical, intellectual, emotional and moral limits, seeking to learn, for example, what are the limits of the human body? What are the limits of the human mind? What are the limits to human suffering? What are the limits to human evil? These limits have been tested in sport, in business, in play, in war, and in love—not with the hope of actually identifying any limits, but rather with the evolutionary goal of transcending all possible limits.

As needed, some among these few have avidly pursued physical, intellectual, psychological and moral enhancements.

Now the option of pursuing these enhancements using genetic technologies is on the horizon and keenly awaited, as is evidenced in the remarks of [molecular biologist] Robert Sinsheimer, an early pioneer of the Human Genome Project:

> It is a new horizon in the history of man. Some may smile and may feel this is but a new version of the old dream, of the perfection of man. It is that, but it is something more. The old dreams of the cultural perfection of man were always sharply constrained by his inherent, inherited imperfections and limitations. Man is all too clearly an imperfect and flawed creature. Considering his evolution, it is hardly likely that he could be otherwise. To foster his better traits and to curb his worse by cultural means has always been, while clearly not impossible, in many instances most difficult. It has been an Archimedean attempt to move the world, but with the short arm of a lever. We now glimpse another route—the chance to ease the internal strains and heal the internal flaws directly, to carry on and consciously perfect far beyond our present vision this remarkable product of two billion years of evolution.

Sinsheimer's hopes are now more imminent than ever.

Here we offer an *avant garde* sketch of human nature. Humans are indeed imperfect creatures, but imperfection is not a necessary condition for humanness. Humans are not merely inquisitive or competitive; rather, we posit that the essential characteristics of humanness are *perfectibility* and the biosocial drive to pursue perfection. These essential characteristics are neither merely naturally present nor culturally driven, but rather biosocially over-determined. We are on the cusp of what may prove to be our final evolutionary stage.

Genetic Enhancement Is Humanity's Destiny

To summarise, there are good reasons to believe that attempts to develop and use genetic enhancement technologies are fraught with moral peril. Nevertheless, in our view, their development and use are inevitable, not simply because of capitalist forces (though these are by no means inconsequential), or because of heedless liberalism (which surely plays a role), or because of a natural desire for knowledge (which is also a significant consideration), or because of a natural or fostered desire to outperform (which, too, is partly explanatory), but also because this is our destiny chosen by those among us who are intent on achieving self-actualisation by controlling the human evolutionary story.

In closing, we maintain that accepting the inevitability of genetic enhancement technologies is an important and necessary step forward in the ethical debate about the development and use of such technologies. We need to change the lens through which we perceive, and therefore approach, the prospect of enhancing humans genetically. In recognising the futility of trying to stop these technologies, we can usefully direct our energies to a systematic analysis of the appropriate scope of their use. The goal of such a project would be to influence how the technologies will be developed, and the individual, social, cultural, political, economic, ecological, and evolutionary ends the technologies should serve. It is to these tasks that bioethical attention must now fully turn.

Genetic Enhancement Is Too Unlikely to Worry About

Steven Pinker

Steven Pinker is a professor of psychology at Harvard University and the author of six books. In the following viewpoint he argues that genetic enhancement of humans is not nearly as likely to occur as either advocates or opponents are assuming. In the first place, he says, there have been many past predictions that have turned out to be wrong, both because they involved technologies that were more difficult to develop than had been expected and because users have weighed the possible benefits against the disadvantages. He explains that genetic enhancement of talents may be impossible because although tens of thousands of genes working together do produce inherited effects, single genes do not; it is the pattern of gene expression that is important. Furthermore, many genes have multiple effects—bad ones along with those that are desired. It is often said that parents will opt for genetic enhancement because they want to give their children every possible advantage; but, Pinker says, they have an even stronger desire not to harm their children, so most will not choose to take the risks genetic enhancement would involve.

This year [2003], the 50th anniversary of the discovery of the structure of DNA has kindled many debates about the implications of that knowledge for the human condition. Arguably the most emotionally charged is the debate over the prospect of human genetic enhancement, or "designer babies." It's only a matter of time, many say, before parents will improve their children's intelligence and personality by having suitable genes inserted into them shortly after conception.

A few commentators have welcomed genetic enhancement as the latest step forward in the age-old struggle to improve human life. But many more are appalled. They warn that it is a Faustian grab at divine powers that will never be used wisely by us mortals. They worry that it will spawn the ultimate form of inequality, a genetic caste system. In his book *Our Posthuman Future* . . . the conservative thinker Francis Fukuyama warns that genetic enhancement will change human nature itself and corrode the notion of a common humanity that undergirds the social order. Bill McKibben, writing from the political left, raises similar concerns in his new jeremiad *Enough: Staying Human in an Engineered Age.*

But whether they welcome or decry it, almost everyone agrees that genetic enhancement is inevitable if research proceeds on its current course. Genetic enhancement is a major concern of the President's Council on Bioethics; its chairman, Leon Kass, and several of its members, including Fukuyama, are outspoken worriers.

As it happens, some kinds of genetic enhancement are already here. Anyone who has been turned down for a date has been a victim of the human drive to exert control over half the genes of one's future children. And it is already possible to test embryos conceived in vitro [outside the body] and select those that are free of genetic defects such as cystic fibrosis.

But when it comes to direct genetic enhancement—engineering babies so they will carry genes for desirable traits—there are many reasons to be skeptical. Not only is genetic enhancement not inevitable, it is not particularly likely in our lifetimes. This skepticism arises from three sources: futurology and its limits, the science of behavioral genetics, and human nature itself.

A Legacy of Failed Predictions

The history of the future should make us raise an eyebrow whenever the experts tell us how we will live 10, 20, or 50 years from now. Not long ago, we were assured that by the turn of the century we would live in domed cities, commute by jet-pack, and clean our homes with nuclear-powered vacuum cleaners wielded by robot maids. More recently we were promised the paperless office, interactive television, the Internet refrigerator, and the end of bricks-and-mortar retail. It's not just that these developments have not yet happened. Many of them, like domed cities, never will happen. Even in mundane cases, technological progress is far from inexorable. Air travel, for example, is barely faster or more comfortable today than it was when commercial jets were introduced 50 years ago.

Why are technological predictions usually wrong? Many futurologists write as if current progress can be extrapolated indefinitely—committing the fallacy of climbing trees to get to the moon. They routinely underestimate how much has to go right for a development to change our lives. It takes more than a single "eureka!" It takes a large number of more boring discoveries, together with the psychological and sociological imponderables that make people adopt some invention en masse. Who could have predicted that the videophones of the 1960s would sink like a stone while the text messaging of the 1990s would become a teenage craze?

Finally, futurologists tend to focus their fantasies on the benefits of a new technology, whereas actual users weigh both the benefits and the costs. Do you really want to take the time to install software upgrades on your refrigerator, or reboot it when it crashes?

Patterns of Genes, Not Single Genes

Many prognosticators assume that we are currently discovering single genes for mathematical giftedness, musical talent, athletic prowess, and the like. The reality is very different. The Achilles' heel of genetic enhancement will be the rarity of single genes with consistent beneficial effects.

Behavioral genetics has uncovered a paradox. We know that tens of thousands of genes working together have a large effect on the mind. Studies show that identical twins (who share all their genes) are more similar than fraternal twins (who share half of those genes that vary from person to person), who in turn are more similar than adopted siblings (who share even fewer of the varying genes). Adoption studies show that children tend to resemble their biological relatives in personality and intelligence more than they resemble their adoptive relatives.

But these are the effects of sharing an entire genome, or half of one. The effects of a *single* gene are much harder to show. Geneticists have failed to find single genes that consistently cause schizophrenia, autism, or manic-depressive disorder, even though these conditions are substantially heritable. And if we can't find a gene for schizophrenia, we're even less likely to find one for humor, musical talent, or likeability, because it's easier to disrupt a complex system with a single defective part than to improve it by adding a single beneficial one. The 1998 report of a gene that was correlated with a 4-point advantage in IQ was recently withdrawn because it did not replicate in a larger sample—a common fate for putative single-gene discoveries.

So don't hold your breath for the literary-creativity gene or the musical-talent gene. The human brain is not a bag of traits with one gene for each trait. Neural development is a staggeringly complex process guided by many genes interacting in feedback loops. The effect of one gene and the effect of a second gene don't produce the sum of their effects when they're simultaneously at work. The *pattern* of expression of genes (when they are turned on or off by proteins and other signals) is as important as which genes are present.

Even when genes should be at their most predictable—in identical twins, who share all their genes, and hence all the interactions among their genes—there are no foregone conclusions about anyone's traits or behavior. Identical twins reared together, who share not only their genes but most of their environment, are imperfectly correlated in personality measures like extroversion and neuroticism. The correlations, to be sure, are much larger than those for fraternal twins or unrelated people, but they are seldom greater than .5. This tells us there is an enormous role for chance in the development of a human being.

Concern for Side Effects

It gets worse. Most genes have multiple effects, and evolution selects those genes that achieve the best compromise between positive and negative impacts. Take the most famous case of genetic enhancement on record: the mice that were given extra copies of the NMDA receptor, which is critical to learning and memory. These poster mice did learn mazes more quickly—but they also turned out to be hypersensitive to pain. Closer to home, there is a gene in humans that may be correlated with a 10-point boost in IQ. But it is also associated with a 10-percent chance of developing torsion dystonia, which can confine the sufferer to a wheelchair with uncontrollable muscle spasms.

So even if genetic enhancement could work in principle, the problem is how to get there from here. How can scientists try out different genes to enhance the minds of babies given that many of those genes could have terrible side effects?

Genetic enhancement faces another problem: Most traits are desirable at intermediate values. Wallis Simpson [the Duchess of Windsor] said that you can't be too rich or too thin, but other traits don't work that way. Take aggressiveness. Parents don't want their children to be punching bags or doormats, but they don't want Attila the Hun, either. Most want their children to face life with confidence rather than sitting at home cowering in fear, but they don't want a reckless daredevil out of [the TV show] "Jackass." So even if a gene had some consistent effect, whether the effect was desirable would depend on what the other tens of thousands of genes in that child are doing.

The third obstacle to re-engineering human nature comes from human nature itself. We are often told that it's only human for parents to give their children every possible advantage. Stereotypical yuppies who play Mozart to their pregnant bellies and bombard their newborns with flash cards would stop at nothing, it is said, to give their children the ultimate head start in life.

But while parents may have a strong desire to help their children, they have an even stronger desire *not to hurt* their children. Playing Mozart may not make a fetus smarter, but it probably won't make it stupider or harm it in other ways. Not so for genetic enhancement. It is not obvious that even the most overinvested parent would accept a small risk of retardation in exchange for a moderate chance of improvement.

Our intuitions about naturalness and contamination are another speed bump on the road to genetically engineered babies. In all cultures, it's widely believed that living things have essences which give them certain powers and which can be contaminated by pollutants. These intuitions have been powerful impediments to the acceptance of various technologies. Many people are repelled by genetically modified foods even though those foods have never been shown to be unsafe or harmful to the environment. If people are repulsed by genetically modified soybeans, would they really welcome genetically modified children?

Unlikely to Change Human Nature

Finally, anyone who has undergone in-vitro fertilization knows that it's a decidedly unpleasant procedure, especially in comparison to sex. Infertile couples may choose it as a last resort, and some kooks may choose it to have a child born under a certain astrological sign or for other frivolous reasons. But people who have the choice generally prefer to conceive their children the old-fashioned way.

It is misleading, then, to assume that parents will soon face the question, "Would you opt for a procedure that would give you a happier and more talented child?" When it's put like that, who would say no? The real question will be, "Would you opt for a traumatic and expensive procedure that might give you a slightly happier and more talented child, or might give you a less happy, less talented child, or might give you a deformed child, and probably would make no difference?" For genetic enhancement to "change human nature," not just a few but *billions* of people would have to answer yes.

My point is not that genetic enhancement is impossible, just that it is far from inevitable. And that has implications. Some bioethicists have called for impeding or criminalizing certain kinds of research in genetics and reproductive medicine, despite their promise of improvement in health and happiness. That is because the research, they say, will inevitably lead to designer babies. If genetic enhancement really were just around the corner, these proposals would have to be taken seriously. But if the prospect is very much in doubt, we can deal with the ethical conundrums if and when they arise. Rather than decrying our posthuman future, thinkers should acknowledge the frailty of technological predictions. They should base policy recommendations on likelihoods rather than fantasies.

Organizations to Contact

Biotechnology Industry Organization (BIO)
1225 Eye St. NW, Suite 400
  Washington, DC 20005
(202) 962-9200
e-mail: info@bio.org
Web sites: www.bio.org and http://science.bio.org

BIO is a trade and lobbying organization for the biotechnology industry, representing companies and academic institutions; it aims to be the champion of biotechnology and the advocate for its member organizations.

Campaign for Responsible Transplantation
PO Box 2751, New York, NY 10163-2751
(212) 579-3477
e-mail: banxeno@yahoo.com
Web site: www.crt-online.org

The Campaign for Responsible Transplantation is a nonprofit organization launched out of concern over the rush to commercialize animal-to-human organ, cell, and tissue transplantation (xenotransplantation). Its international coalition includes over ninety public interest groups. It seeks a total ban on xenotransplantation.

Campaign to Label Genetically Engineered Foods
PO Box 55699, Seattle, WA 98155
(425) 771-4049 • fax: (425) 740-8967
e-mail: label@thecampaign.org
Web site: www.thecampaign.org

This is a political organization that aims to create a national grassroots consumer campaign for the purpose of lobbying Congress and the president to pass legislation that will require the labeling of genetically engineered foods in the United States. Its Web site contains links to many organizations and other sites focused on biotechnology in agriculture.

Center for Bioethics and Human Dignity
2065 Half Day Rd., Bannockburn, IL 60015
(847) 317-8180 • fax: (847) 317-8101
e-mail: info@cbhd.org
Web site: www.cbhd.org

The Center for Bioethics and Human Dignity is a nonprofit organization that exists to help individuals and organizations address pressing bioethical challenges, including managed care, end-of-life treatment, genetic intervention, euthanasia and suicide, and reproductive technologies.

Center for Genetics and Society
436 Fourteenth St., Suite 700
   Oakland, CA 94612
(510) 625-0819 • fax: (510) 625-0874
Web site: www.genetics-and-society.org

The Center for Genetics and Society is a nonprofit information and public affairs organization working to encourage responsible uses and effective societal governance of the new human genetic and reproductive technologies. It works with a network of scientists, health professionals, civil society leaders, and others. Its Web site contains a large amount of informational material.

Council for Responsible Genetics
5 Upland Rd., Suite 3, Cambridge, MA 02140
(617) 868-0870 • fax: (617) 491-5344
e-mail: crg@gene-watch.org
Web site: www.gene-watch.org

The Council for Responsible Genetics is a nonprofit, nongovernmental organization that fosters public debate about the social, ethical, and environmental implications of genetic technologies. It publishes the bimonthly magazine *GeneWatch*, and partial archives can be found at its Web site.

Genetic Alliance
4301 Connecticut Ave. NW, Suite 404,
   Washington, DC 20008-2369
(202) 966-5557 • fax: (202) 966-8553
e-mail: info@geneticalliance.org
Web site: www.geneticalliance.org

Genetic Alliance is an international coalition comprised of more than six hundred advocacy, research, and health care organizations that represent millions of individuals with genetic conditions and their interests. It aims to improve the climate for the development of technologies that will ultimately lead to improved human health.

Genetically Engineered Organisms Public Issues Education Project (GEO-PIE)
Cornell Cooperative Extension
   Ithaca, NY 14853-5905
(607) 255-2291 • fax: (607) 255-0788
e-mail: jes30@cornell.edu
Web site: www.geo-pie.cornell.edu

GEO-PIE is a project of Cornell University. It was developed to create objective educational materials that explore the complex scientific and social issues associated with genetic engineering. Its Web site contains a great deal of information on the subject, including media and expert opinion.

Genetic ID
PO Box 1810, Fairfield, IA 52556-9030
(877) 384-6193 • fax: (641) 472-9198
e-mail: info@genetic-id.com
Web site: www.genetic-id.com

Genetic ID conducts testing of genetically modified organisms (GMOs) for agricultural and food industry clients. The organization also helps its clients grow and sustain their markets and exports, guiding them through various countries' government regulations and procedures.

Genetics Policy Institute
11924 Forest Hill Blvd., Suite 22
  Wellington, FL   33414-6258
(888) 238-1423 • fax: (561) 791-3889
Web site: www.genpol.org

The Genetics Policy Institute is a leading nonprofit organization dedicated to establishing a positive legal framework to advance the search for cutting-edge cures. Its Web site maintains press releases related to the institute's work.

GeneWatch UK
The Mill House, Manchester Rd.
  Tideswell, Buxton, Derbyshire, UK SK17 8LN
e-mail: mail@genewatch.org
Web site: www.genewatch.org

GeneWatch UK aims to ensure that genetic technologies are developed and used in the public interest and in a way that promotes human health, protects the environment, and respects human rights and the interests of animals. Its Web site contains material about all types of genetic engineering.

Hastings Center
21 Malcolm Gordon Rd.
  Garrison, NY 10524-5555
(845) 424-4040 • fax: (845) 424-4545
e-mail: mail@thehastingscenter.org
Web site: www.thehastingscenter.org

The Hastings Center is an independent, nonpartisan, and nonprofit bioethics research institute that explores fundamental and emerging questions in health care, biotechnology, and the environment. It publishes many books and papers, as well as the bimonthly *Hastings Center Report*, which includes essays, commentary, and scholarly articles.

International Center for Technology Assessment (CTA)
660 Pennsylvania Ave. SE, Suite 302
  Washington, DC   20003
(202) 547-9359 • fax: (202) 547-9429
e-mail: info@icta.org
Web site: www.icta.org

The International Center for Technology Assessment is a nonprofit, bipartisan organization committed to providing the public with full assessments and analyses of technology's impact on society. CTA is devoted to fully exploring the economic, ethical, social, environmental, and political impacts that can result from the applications of technology or technological systems. The center has taken a stand against human cloning and argues for limits on genetic engineering.

President's Council on Bioethics
1801 Pennsylvania Ave. NW, Suite 700
    Washington, DC 20006
(202) 296-4669
e-mail: info@bioethics.gov
Web site: www.bioethics.gov

This council advises the president of the United States on ethical issues related to advances in biomedical science and technology. Its reports—some book length—are available at the council's Web site.

World Transhumanist Association
PO Box 128, Willington, CT 06279
(860) 297-2376 • fax: (860) 297-4136
e-mail: secretary@transhumanism.org
Web site: http://transhumanism.org

The World Transhumanist Association is an international nonprofit membership organization which advocates the ethical use of technology to expand human capacities. It believes that emerging technologies such as genetic engineering will have a powerful role in improving the quality of life.

Bibliography

Books

John C. Avise · *The Hope, Hype, and Reality of Genetic Engineering* . New York: Oxford University Press, 2004.

Britt Bailey and Marc Lappe, eds. · *Engineering the Farm: The Social and Ethical Aspects of Agricultural Biotechnology*. Washington, DC: Island Press, 2002.

Ronald Bailey · *Liberation Biology: The Scientific and Moral Case for the Biotech Revolution.* Amherst, NY: Prometheus, 2005.

Harold W. Baille and Timothy K. Casey, eds. · *Is Human Nature Obsolete? Genetics, Bioengineering, and the Future of the Human Condition.* Cambridge, MA: MIT Press, 2005.

M.W. Bauer and G. Gaskell, eds. · *Biotechnology: The Making of a Global Controversy.* New York: Cambridge University Press, 2002.

Aluízio Borém, Fabrício R. Santos, and David E. Bowen · *Understanding Biotechnology.* Upper Saddle River, NJ: Prentice-Hall, 2003.

Rick J. Carlson and Gary Stimeling · *The Terrible Gift: The Brave New World of Genetic Medicine.* New York: Public Affairs, 2002.

Ronald Cole-Turner, ed. · *Beyond Cloning: Religion and the Remaking of Humanity.* Harrisburg, PA: Trinity, 2001.

Elaine Dewar

The Second Tree: Stem Cells, Clones, Chimeras, and Quests for Immortality. New York: Carroll & Graf, 2004.

John H. Evans

Playing God? Human Genetic Engineering and the Rationalization of Public Bioethical Debate. Chicago: University of Chicago Press, 2002.

Francis Fukuyama

Our Posthuman Future: Consequences of the Biotechnical Revolution. New York: Farrar, Straus & Giroux, 2002.

Michael Fumento

Bioevolution: How Biotechnology Is Changing Our World. San Francisco: Encounter, 2003.

Joel Garreau

Radical Evolution: The Promise and Peril of Enhancing Our Minds, Our Bodies—and What It Means to Be Human. New York: Doubleday, 2005.

Kathleen Hart

Eating in the Dark: America's Experiment with Genetically Engineered Food. New York: Vintage, 2003.

James Hughes

Citizen Cyborg: Why Democratic Societies Must Respond to the Redesigned Human of the Future. Cambridge, MA: Westview, 2004.

Leon R. Kass

Life, Liberty, and the Defense of Dignity: The Challenge for Bioethics. San Francisco: Encounter, 2002.

Sheldon Krimsky and Peter Shorett

Rights and Liberties in the Biotech Age: Why We Need a Genetic Bill of Rights. Lanham, MD: Rowman & Littlefield, 2005.

David Magnus, Arthur L. Caplan, and Glenn McGee, eds.	*Who Owns Life?* Amherst, NY: Prometheus, 2002.
Bill McKibben	*Enough: Staying Human in an Engineered Age.* New York: Henry Holt, 2003.
Maxwell J. Mehlman	*Wondergenes: Genetic Enhancement and the Future of Society.* Bloomington: Indiana University Press, 2003.
Henry J. Miller and Gregory Conko	*The Frankenfood Myth.* Westport, CT: Praeger, 2004.
Ramez Naam	*More than Human: Embracing the Promise of Biological Enhancement.* New York: Broadway, 2005.
President's Council on Bioethics	*Beyond Therapy: Biotechnology and the Pursuit of Happiness.* New York: Regan, 2003. www.bioethics.gov/reports/beyondtherapy.
Matt Ridley	*Nature Via Nurture: Genes, Experience and What Makes Us Human.* New York: HarperCollins, 2003. Reprinted as *The Agile Gene.* New York. Harper-Perennial, 2004.
Michael Ruse and David Castle, eds.	*Genetically Modified Foods: Debating Biotechnology.* Amherst, NY: Prometheus, 2002.
Wesley J. Smith	*Consumer's Guide to a Brave New World.* San Francisco: Encounter, 2004.

Gregory Stock   *Redesigning Humans: Our Inevitable Genetic Future.* Boston: Houghton Mifflin, 2002.

Brian Tokar, ed.   *Redesigning Life? The Worldwide Challenge to Genetic Engineering.* New York: Zed, 2001.

Mark L. Winston   *Travels in the Genetically Modified Zone.* Cambridge, MA: Harvard University Press, 2002.

Periodicals

Catherine Arnst   "Aging Is Becoming So Yesterday," *Business Week,* October 11, 2004.

Ronald Bailey   "Shimmering Chimeras," *Reason,* December 24, 2003.

Michael Behar   "Will Genetics Destroy Sports?" *Discover,* July 2004.

David Bjerklie and Alice Park   "How Doctors Help the Dopers," *Time,* August 16, 2004.

Stewart Brand   "Environmental Heresies," *Technology Review,* May 2005.

Linda Bren   "Genetic Engineering: The Future of Foods?" *FDA Consumer,* November 2003.

Maria Cavazzana-Calvo et al.   "The Future of Gene Therapy," *Nature,* February 26, 2004.

Erika Check   "RNA to the Rescue?" *Nature,* September 4, 2003.

Gerald D. Coleman — "Is Genetic Engineering the Answer to Hunger?" *America*, February 21, 2005.

Barry Commoner — "The Spurious Foundation of Genetic Engineering," *Harper's*, February 2002.

Clive Cookson — "Mother of All Cells," *Scientific American*, July 2005.

Claire Hope Cummings — "Trespass," *World Watch*, January 2005.

Alyssa Ford — "Humanity the Remix," *Utne Reader*, May 2005.

R.P. Freckleton et al. — "Deciding the Future of GM Crops in Europe," *Science*, November 7, 2003.

David H. Freedman — "Reinventing the Mouse," *Newsweek*, June 30–July 7, 2003.

Henry Fountain — "For Zebrafish, That Certain Glow," *New York Times*, February 1, 2005.

Joel Garreau — "Perfecting the Human," *Fortune*, May 30, 2005.

W. Wayt Gibbs — "Synthetic Life," *Scientific American*, May 2004.

Alexandra M. Goho — "Life Made to Order," *Technology Review*, April 2003.

Fred Guterl et al. — "The Fear of Food," *Newsweek*, January 27, 2003.

Ernie Hood — "RNAi: What's All the Noise About

Gene Silencing?" *Environmental Health Perspectives,* March 2004.

David Kupfer — "The Genetic Resistance," *Earth Island Journal,* Summer 2004.

Steven Luff — "Dabbling with DNA," *Delicious Living,* March 2005.

Charles C. Mann — "New and Improved!" *Wired,* April 2003.

Lorne McClinton — "Fields of Green," *Canadian Business,* March 28, 2005.

Sean McDonagh — "Genetic Engineering Is Not the Answer," *America,* May 2, 2005.

Bill McKibben and Stephanie Kratt — "Design-a-Kid," *Christian Century,* May 17, 2003.

Henry I. Miller and Gregory Conko — "Biotech and Baby Food," *Policy Review,* June 2003.

Patrick Moore — "The Green Case for Biotech," *American Enterprise,* March 2004.

Steve Nash — "The Phantom Forest: Research on Gene-Altered Trees Leaps Ahead, into a Regulatory Limbo," *Bioscience,* May 2003.

Robin Orwant — "What Makes Us Human?" *New Scientist,* February 21, 2004.

Robert Paarlberg — "From the Green Revolution to the Gene Revolution," *Environment,* January 2005

Adam Piore et al.   "What Green Revolution?" *Newsweek*, September 15, 2003.

Jonathan Rauch   "Will Frankenfood Save the Planet?" *Atlantic Monthly*, October 2003.

Craig Simons   "Of Rice and Men," *Newsweek*, December 20, 2004.

John Simons   "The Quest for Custom Cures," *Fortune*, May 2, 2005.

H. Lee Sweeney   "Gene Doping," *Scientific American*, July 2004.

Liz Szabo   "Gene Therapy Runs into Roadblocks," *USA Today*, April 4, 2005.

Nicholas Wade   "Chimeras on the Horizon, but Don't Expect Centaurs," *New York Times*, May 3, 2005.

Index